SCANDINAVIAN
PAINTED FURNITURE

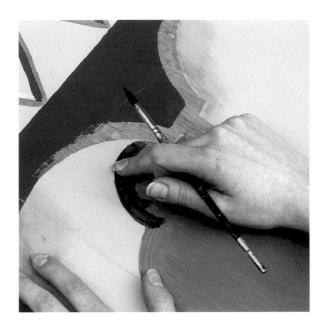

SCANDINAVIAN PAINTED FURNITURE
A STEP-BY-STEP WORKBOOK

Jocasta Innes and Suzanne Martin

Special Photography by
Mark Gatehouse

CASSELL

A CASSELL BOOK
First published in 1994
Reprinted in 1995
Cassell Publishers Ltd
Wellington House
125 Strand
London
WC2R 0BB

Text copyright © Jocasta Innes 1994
Volume rights and captions copyright © 1994 Cassell
First paperback edition 1997

Distributed in the United States by
Sterling Publishers Co. Inc
387 Park Avenue South, New York, NY10016-8810

British Library Cataloguing-in-Publication Data
A catalogue record for this book is available from the British Library

ISBN 0-304-35013-3

Design, editing and reproduction by
Blackjacks Ltd, London

Printed and bound in Hong Kong by Dah Hua Printing Press Co.

Photo Acknowledgements
Page 25 from *Dekorativ Målning* by Pontus Tunander, ICA Bokförlag Västerås 1988
Page 36 from *Korgmålning för och nu* by Anita Gunnars, ICA Bokförlag Västerås 1989
Page 112 from *Stolar* by Lars, Ursular and Sven Nilsson, ICA Bokförlag Västerås 1993

Acknowledgements
The publishers gratefully acknowledge the assistance of Lena Nessle in making available copyright
photographs and paint recipes from her publications as follows: photographs on pages 43, 47, 58, 124, 130
from *Måla som förr, folkligt och friskt*, Stockholm 1992; paint recipes on page 154 from
Måla inomhus på gammalt vis, Stockholm 1985.

Contents

Introduction
Painted Furniture in Scandinavia

The Swedes have a saying 'the forest is the poor man's shirt', a pithy and picturesque comment on the importance of timber in the history, both collective and individual, of the five countries (Norway, Finland, Sweden, Denmark and Iceland) which make up the Nordic federation. Not that the point needs much underlining, since reminders of what has been called 'the conifer culture' are everywhere: whole buildings, vigorous carved porches, stave churches, and a legacy of wonderful wooden furniture and artefacts as rich and varied as anywhere in the world.

Conifer (cone-bearing) trees (pine, fir, spruce) yield timber that is technically classified as softwood, as distinct from hardwoods like oak, mahogany, iroko. A joiner or carpenter will tell you more about the personality of softwoods as a working material. They are easy to cut, but – with the exception of yellow pine, which is not native to Scandinavia – difficult to carve, tending to chip and flake. Carved ornaments have to be shallow, not undercut, and quite simply even crude in design. Knots and 'shakes' – splits across the grain – are a problem too, though one less often encountered in the good old days when timber was left to grow for perhaps a century, close packed to discourage branching and its accompanying

knots, then seasoned properly to dry out the resinous content gradually, thus guarding against shrinking, warping and other problems which characterise today's fast-grown cash crops. Softwoods are also especially attractive to borers, whose burrowing can reduce a chair leg to a frail honeycomb indicated on the surface only by a slight peppering of tiny holes.

What makes pre-twentieth-century Scandinavian softwood furniture so uniquely appealing to modern taste is that, with very few exceptions, it was always given a finishing coat of paint.

Painting Softwood Furniture

There were many reasons why softwood furniture was invariably painted the length and breadth of Scandinavia; and it was not just free-standing pieces which were painted, but also fitments like cupboard beds, built-in shelving and dressers. The painting sheds interesting light on the societies which commissioned or bought such pieces. Softwoods, to people surrounded by as many conifers as there are herrings in the Baltic, were too commonplace to be interesting or appealing in themselves, unadorned. Just as the classical Greeks painted marble and the medieval English painted stone, so the people of Scandinavia

opposite
This corner of an old farm kitchen/living room sums up most of the essential features of Scandinavian peasant interiors; bare scrubbed boards, a vivid blue paint used on built-in cupboards and plate racks, a snatch of wall painting and even an antique spindle.

left
From the homely to the sublime. The mirrored room in King Gustav III's exquisite Haga Pavilion is one of the great interiors of the world. A Nordic version of a Greek temple whose antique marble columns, inset with glass, overlook a lake which reflects light back on to the walls.

chose to paint their ubiquitous timbers. There may have been a preservationist motive, too: an idea that layers of paint would deter beetles, as well as guarding against dirt and grime and wear and tear. Some old Scandinavian paint formulas contain vitriol and lime, both of which deter insect parasites.

The most convincing explanation for the painting, however, is the more humanly appealing one that the added colour and drama which painted finishes supply were an end in themselves, the most immediate tonic for senses dulled or depressed by the notoriously long northern winters, where daylight may last a brief hour or two. 'Snow-light', the reflected daylight from deep snow outside, though relied upon by a thrifty peasantry before the advent of electricity,

can also cast a chilly glare which cries out for what Carl Larsson (author of *Etthem,* the world famous chronicle of Swedish aristocratic family life) called 'hearty' colour.

Peasant societies everywhere make a parade of bright colour in their costumes, artefacts and homes. It is striking that the favoured colour in peasant dress throughout Scandinavia is a ringing scarlet, the most vivid contrast to the white/blue/grey monotony of their wintry landscape. Scarlet enters much less into painted work, but this may well be because the pigment needed to colour a paint scarlet was more costly than the dyes needed to colour a fabric. This is still the case even today, when most pigment is synthetic. However, the cheaper reds, the brownreds mixed with iron oxides, seem to have been universally popular, both as exterior and interior paint and both as a background to applied decoration and an integral part of it.

Peasant Furniture

There is an important distinction to be made between two quite different approaches to furniture painting and decoration as they developed in Scandinavia. There is the rural, peasant type of decoration ('folk' is a word frowned upon by modern scholars), distinguished by strong colours, a wealth of surface decoration and an intensely regional, often local character. The same characteristics are to be found in peasant

top
Checks, gilding, Rococo flower borders and a trompe-l'œil *dado add up to a quintessentially Swedish vignette.*

left
Decorated painted 'panels' were fashionable in the later part of the eighteenth century as wall treatments. Against this background the freshness of striped ticking upholstery adds a typically understated charm to the long sofa.

left
Though the furniture in this
room is basic, it is all of a
certain elegance, painted white
like the boarded ceiling to
maximize light. However, it is
the sprightly and colourful wall
paintings which dress up the
room and transform it into a
party piece.

costume but, whereas it might have been acceptable for a native of Dalarna or Jämtland to acquire, say, a clock from Mora (its painted longcase clocks were much coveted), it would have been as outrageous to dress in the costume of a neighbouring village as to play football today in the colours of another team. Peasant painted furniture and decoration share other characteristics. A regional style or typical colour scheme, once laid down, is then faithfully copied in its essentials by succeeding generations of painters and craftsmen, whether professional, itinerant or do-it-oneselfers. In other words, painters were content to work within an inherited regional repertoire of motifs and colours. From time to time, though, some individual painter's skills, facility or discovery of a new-fangled (which usually meant several decades behind the latest fashion) flourish led to improvements or embellishments on the basic themes. But, by and large, peasant art is not notable for its originality nor what is generally referred to as self-expression. On the other hand skill in execution varied considerably. Where the names of individual artists have been recorded, this was probably an acknowledgement of a local reputation. Also, some regional styles of decoration, such as the Norwegian 'rosmålning', or the

'clouds marbling' of Swedish Hälsingland, or the 'kurbits' painting of Dalarna, became known and sought after over a much wider area than the region where they originated. However, an expert in this field can almost always fix the provenance and date of a particular piece on sight. The experts will also tell you the most idiosyncratic decoration evolves in regions furthest from big cities and seaports and so least exposed to cosmopolitan ideas and fashions.

'Gentlemanly' Furniture

The other style of painted furniture associated with Scandinavia, and Sweden in particular, is altogether different, as much in its use of paint and colour as in its shape and function. This is what might be called 'gentlemanly' furniture, making a similar distinction to that made by Swedes between peasant farms and gentleman farms. This furniture was made for upper-class homes, from the relatively modest but charming wooden villas occupied by the urban middle class to the grand houses and castles of the nobility. In this social class, educated and travelled, wider European fashions and standards were familiar and influential, though their expression in Scandinavian interiors and furnishings tended to lag behind by a decade or so

such centres of creative activity as Paris and London, Berlin and St. Petersburg. Broadly speaking, however, the styles and spirit of Baroque, Rococo and Neoclassicism were repeated in the interiors of contemporary middle- and upper-class Scandinavian homes. But though the aesthetic vocabulary remained much the same, it was delivered with a distinctly Scandinavian accent. Pale board floors were more common than Aubusson carpets, painted 'tapeter' than imported tapestries, silk hangings or panels of imitation lacquer. When it came to furniture, the striking difference was that, while in shape and function it frequently imitated foreign models, it was invariably made of softwood and invariably painted.

above
Although unmistakably rustic, this little bedroom has pretensions to elegance, as revealed by the formal wall painting and striped runner.

The paint treatments used on this class of furniture were restrained in their use of colour and applied decoration and technically sophisticated. By the mid eighteenth century, soft colours had become fashionable; these included blue-green, putty, pale-straw yellow, which were finished with fine glazes and combined with gold leaf. A fine example of such decoration can be seen on the Rococo Swedish writing-table on p.83. Chairs of this period tend to be round-backed and upholstered – the 'ros-stol' – while most pieces had elegantly splayed, tapering legs. Compared with much contemporary European work, with its carved detail, the general appearance of this Scandinavian furniture is simple, refined and charming in its elegant lines and gentle colouring, characteristics which make it particularly appealing to twentieth-century taste.

Swedish Neoclassicism

It is, however, the late eighteenth-century, Neo-classical style, christened 'Gustaviansk' after the talented, but ill-fated, King Gustav III of Sweden, who corresponded with Marie Antoinette about his decorating projects, which seems to have struck deepest into Scandinavian sensibilities and still exercises a lingering influence. The curvaceous lines and decorative flourishes of the Rococo modulate here into something more rectilinear; splayed legs become straight though finely tapering, chairs have straight backs, the typical long narrow sofas are of a thoroughbred purity of line, and exquisitely uncomfortable. Mirrors, so popular throughout the Nordic countries because of their power of reflecting and multiplying candlelight, became longer and rectangular instead of round or oval.

One can hazard many guesses as to why this stripped purity of line struck such a responsive chord in Scandinavia. Perhaps people thought pieces modelled – even distantly – on the furniture of Ancient Greece and Rome would outlast the caprices of mere fashion. Certainly, its clarity of line looked well in the typically pastel interiors of the period,

right
The vivid contrasts of rich colour shown in this vignette are typical of Denmark, by far the most cosmopolitan of the Scandinavian countries.

with their newly enlarged windows looped and draped *à la grecque* with folds of translucent muslin. Another, more down-to-earth explanation must surely be that softwood is better adapted to straight up-and-down shapes; straight legs for instance, are stronger than splayed ones, as well as being easier to cut and shape. But this purity was always redeemed from austerity by paint finishes of delicate charm – pearl grey was the universally popular shade – and by small carved flourishes, ribbons and bows and floral topknots on chair-backs, mirror-frames, cupboards and the like. Often these were picked out in chalky pastel shades: blues, pinks, pale-green and straw-yellow, for contrast. Gold leaf was used less than during the Rococo period, though it still added a subdued richness of effect.

Country Styles

As high style moved out from the centres of Scandinavian fashion, on to country estates or into gentleman farms and middle-class villas, it became 'provincial', with all the local eccentricities and occasional gaucherie that this term implies. Some of the most appealing Scandinavian furniture of the eighteenth and early nineteenth centuries belongs to this genre. The fine bombé-fronted console or cabinet shown on p.19 is a typical example; this is a rustic interpretation of a sophisticated piece in softwood, simple and generous in shape rather than elegant and given the simplest of painted finishes. The plain garnet-red, however, is made special by the skill with which it was applied, before glazing and varnishing. Such pieces, possibly the work of an estate carpenter, seem to an outside eye to be the strongest expression of provincial style in Scandinavia. They are honest and substantial in their interpretation of an unfamiliar shape in a familiar local material, and they have a noble simplicity which goes beyond the mere aping of gentility. They can look just as much at home in a flat in a high-rise block in Stockholm, as in one of the most perfect small country houses of the Swedish Baroque.

section 2

Brushes and Equipment
A Brief Overview

Brushes

It is never worth buying a cheap brush. Good-quality brushes repay the investment if you take care of them. Cheap brushes are a false economy, as errant hairs appear in your paint work. You then have to stop to prise them off the surface and redo the area because of the mark made. Decorating brushes have strange names; they fall into different categories depending on their size and the stiffness of the bristles. Always use the brush that is appropriate for the job in hand.

Artist's brushes These come in many different shapes and the best are those made from sable bristles. They are used for fine detail. Special liners are used for making thin lines; the bristles are cut diagonally across the ends.

Decorator's brushes The best are made from pig's bristles. The most popular are flat brushes in sizes from 1 in. (2.5cm) to about 6 in. (15cm) across. Oval brushes are rare but they hold more paint.

Dusting brushes Used to stipple out any visible brushstrokes, these are sometimes referred to as softeners. The ends of the bristles are the part used to smooth the paint to a perfect finish. They can also be used to remove dust from the base coat before the glaze is applied.

Fitches Stiff-bristled artist's brushes, they come in a variety of shapes and are necessary for painting and picking out details. The round fitches hold more paint and are very useful for all sorts of work. Fitches can be used for spattering over small areas.

Floggers These are special brushes with long flexible bristles used for dragging and flogging. The flogger is really the only brush that produces the desired result. As it is expensive, a dusting brush can be used instead, but the finish isn't as defined.

Gliders Soft brushes that hold less paint, making them ideal for applying a thin wash of glaze.

Overgrainers Many different brushes can be used to reproduce the grainy look of wood. The bristles are divided up into a number of tiny brushes on the one ferrule to represent the grain.

Stencilling brushes Short squat round brushes with tightly packed bristles.

Stipplers Brushes with a wide end area used to remove specks of glaze in stippling.

Varnishing brushes These have more bristles to the square centimetre than regular decorator's brushes and they should be used only with varnish – any paint residue left in them will spoil your subsequent work. They leave a smooth finish with no visible brushstrokes.

Caring For Your Brushes

As soon as the work is finished, you must clean your brushes. If you have been using water-based paints, then simply clean them thoroughly in soap and warm water. Detergents dry them out. Lather the soap up so that you can get right down to the roots (the ferrule). Rinse thoroughly in running water, then shake to get most of the water off. Small brushes can be stored upside down in a jar, but bigger brushes are better stored suspended from a hook so the air circulating keeps them from mildewing and the bristles don't dry splayed out. To keep the bristle shape in the long term, wrap them in paper and secure with a rubber band. Stencil brushes and other round brushes should always be stored this way. Never leave brushes stored lying down.

Oil-based paints are cleaned off with white spirit or a commercial brush cleaner. Then continue as before by thoroughly rinsing in water and storing the brush carefully.

If you are leaving the work for just an hour or two, keep the bristles moist in foil or in a rag dampened with water or turpentine (depending on the paint).

above

1 Badger Hair Softener 2 Cotton Stockinette 3 Hog Hair Softener 4 Natural Sponge 5 Indian Hog Hair Flogging Brush 6 Fitches 7 Mottler 8 Glider/Varnishing Brush 9 Stencilling Brush 10 Dragging Brush 11 Artist's Brushes 12 Decorator's Brushes 13 Spoons for Mixing 14 Stippling Brush 15 Metal Comb

left

The sort of equipment that the more sophisticated nineteenth-century Scandinavian painter carried from job to job.

Mixing Containers

Small saucers, plastic yoghurt pots and microwave cookware are all handy for mixing small amounts of paint or for decanting when stencilling. For large amounts, when mixing emulsion, for example, you may need to buy a plastic bucket or a paint kettle. Mixing glazes also requires a container large enough to mix one coat at a time. If the work is going to take several days, the container must have an air-tight lid to prevent a skin from forming.

To transfer paint from one receptacle to another, use either a plastic funnel or a ladle. If you are worried about mixing to a given ratio, use a spoon and wipe it clean after use.

Paint and Colour

The Scandinavian Palette

When people talk about characteristically Scandinavian colours they are usually referring to the subtle, glaucous blue-greys and grey-greens that turn up on so much painted furniture, especially from the Gustavian period. In fact, most of the paint colours used in the Nordic countries have a special quality, for which many explanations have been advanced. Scandinavian paint tends to look chalky and 'lean'; one rarely sees a glossy surface on old paintwork. Varnishes appear to have been used infrequently which would help account for this.

In spite of these factors, much antique paint has weathered remarkably well in Scandinavia. Its longevity may have something to do with the dry climate; textiles, for instance, survive exceptionally well and many old houses retain their original eighteenth- and nineteenth-century hangings. Another

reason may be the thoroughness of the paint application. The old prescription that many thin coats are better than few thick ones must have been conscientiously followed. Then, again, powdered pigment was the common tinting agent. Because it was ground by hand, with a muller and stone, the particles tended to be less finely and evenly crushed than they would be in a mechanical process, and this irregularity, while hardly visible to the naked eye, is thought to be more light reflective and hence to give a special resonance to the colours mixed from powder pigment.

Another quality of much old Scandinavian paintwork is transparency. The grain of the wood beneath tends to show through slightly, contributing its own texture. This is so much a characteristic that modern painters working with old or reproduction pieces deliberately imitate it by thinning their paints – usually water-based today for health and ecological reasons – and rubbing them back with fine sandpaper. But they are careful to seal the bare wood first with one or more coats of shellac, to prevent the water paint raising the grain and to avoid colour being absorbed unevenly. The transparency of old oil-based paint finishes is sometimes explained by the fact that the chalky filler used to give body and opacity has gradually absorbed its linseed oil content and become more transparent over time. Whether this was intentional or fortuitous, the results are pleasing and give painted pieces a refinement that makes more conventional paintwork look thick and pasty.

left

A vignette showing a corner of an old painted and decorated cupboard of some pretensions. The thundery blues and rich, earthy reds illustrated on this piece, are very typical of Scandinavian peasant furniture.

right

This simple but fine piece lies somewhere between the high style and vernacular furniture produced by Scandinavian craftsmen in the eighteenth and nineteenth centuries. Although based on European cabinets, it retains a native sturdiness, raised to elegance by a rich glazed red paint finish.

Thin tinted glazes seem to have been a standard finishing material, though invariably only over the best work. Swedish painters seem to have been especially skilful in their use of glazes, which were not by any means always the standard 'antiquing' mixture of raw umber or burnt sienna. On yellow paint they often used a glaze tinted with 'English red', a soft red oxide, to add a subtle glow. On the deep blues and greens which feature on so much painted furniture, their glazes were almost black, imparting the moody or thundery cast which is much admired and copied today. While working on projects for this book I discovered that a transparent olive or drab green washed over a pale grey-green gives a particularly soft and flattering result. Discoveries like these would have become part of a painter's secret repertoire of effects, contributing to his individual style and appeal. These glazes were used by the peasant artists as much as by those working on fine furniture for aristocratic or wealthy clients. It seems probable, though, in this as in so much else, that the idea was first developed by more sophisticated painters, after which it gradually worked its way down through the hierarchy. The 'folk' painters were certainly quick to seize on the use of a glaze finish, in their case principally as a quick way of mellowing and blending together coloured decoration that looked 'jumpy', too sharply contrasted and crudely bright. Innate taste operates at many levels.

In trying to identify the colours that seem most characteristic in Scandinavian painted decoration on furniture, it might help to begin by identifying which colours were uncharacteristic. Scarlet and vermilion are rarely seen; the typical Scandinavian red has a brownish cast, most readily identified on the count- less wooden exteriors treated with 'falun rott', the extraordinarily tough exterior paint (they claim it lasts for up to thirty years) made by tinting a base of lime and casein with red oxide. This rich shade appears constantly on peasant furniture, nicely balancing blues, browns and off-whites, much less often on grander pieces, though I well remember a handsome bombe-front cabinet or commode, provincial rather than rustic in style, given a finish based on this shade but warmed and glazed to a dark garnet red. Sharp pastels are equally rare, whether of the Robert Adam variety, or of the more flamboyant type we associate with Mediterranean décor.

Consciously or unconsciously, a painters' palette is conditioned by light and climate; the hot pinks, lime greens and aquamarine blues that are tamed by a Mediterranean sun would set one's teeth on edge in a Nordic climate. Scandinavian light, in the spring and summer, is as clear and dazzling as in Greece, but it is a silvery, cool light. What one might call 'sophisticated' colours – buff, black or near black, drab olive, lemon-yellow, greenish brown, all of which occur frequently in English eighteenth-century painted furniture – are uncommon in Scandinavia. Overwhelmingly, the favoured shades for grand Gustavian-style furniture seem to be silvery grey, a soft wheat-yellow and a range of gentle, mysterious greyed blues and greens, often contrasted with a gleam of gold leaf or with each other.

The peasant palette is heartier, undoubtedly, but tends to favour the strong dark shades of the Baroque period – deep blue, green, red-brown – for backgrounds to more vivid passages of decoration. Perhaps the most persistent pastel shade used in peasant decoration is a cerulean blue, often found in

Skane in the south of Sweden, combined with brown-red, white, yellow and green. Being closer to the rest of Europe, it seems likely that this jaunty, pretty bouquet of colours may owe something to German folk painting of the 'bauern-malerei' sort and its characteristic motifs of hearts, roses, sprightly birds and much Rococo scroll-work.

Some colours available in Scandinavian paint ranges are interestingly different. One is Dala blue,

Paint formulas for a range of Scandinavian colours are given below. The proportions are not precise and it is advisable – as well as enjoyable – to practise and experiment on fillets of wood.

White with 5 per cent oxide red

White with 10 per cent black, 5 per cent oxide red

Chartreuse yellow with 10 per cent white, 2 per cent black

Chartreuse yellow with 50 per cent white

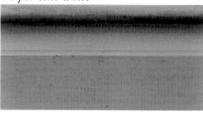

White with 10 per cent raw (green) umber

White with 10 per cent Prussian blue, 5 per cent black

White with 20 per cent cerulean blue

White with 50 per cent yellow ochre

Dala blue with 16 per cent white

Yellow ochre with 70 per cent white

Mars orange with 10 per cent black

White with 20 per cent Prussian blue, 10 per cent black

White with 2 per cent black

the blue favoured by painters in that highly creative centre of regional work. It is a mid-blue, somewhat resembling cobalt, but more vivid and without the green cast of Prussian blue or the purple tinge of ultramarine. Another appealing shade, a dusky purple-brown with a red tinge, goes by the macabre name of Caput Mortuum, 'death's head'.

In my experience, Scandinavian paints in whatever medium are exceptionally intense and true. Unfortunately, these excellent paints are not widely distributed. The most widely available and satisfactory substitute for serious painters and decorators is good-quality dry or powdered pigment. Another, which I mention a bit diffidently since this may look like self-advertisement, might be my own Paint Magic range of Woodwash paints, which Suzanne Martin has used on many of her projects. She liked the colours (though she felt the need for a stronger yellow and a softer blue), especially the chalky texture which rubs back much more satisfactorily than a standard emulsion water-based paint. It also lends itself to being applied, thinned with water, as a transparent paint in the style referred to above.

A stroll through any Scandinavian city confronts a visitor with a perhaps unexpected survival of traditional styles in a culture largely dedicated to modernism, efficiency and a high standard of living. One sees colours on old buildings of a glorious intensity: ochre-yellow, garnet red and, most striking of all, a luminous saffron orange-yellow, not harsh but vivid in a gentle way. These are all traditional limewash colours, used on exteriors since time immemorial, but rarely to be found in countries where so-called 'primitive' paints have been superseded by commercial ranges of exterior paints formulated for speed and efficiency, among other qualities. Limewash colours offer a soft but vivid intensity of colour, darkened by rain, lightened by sun, which seems mobile and delicate compared with the solid tints achieved by hi-tech exterior paint.

Scandinavia continued using these limewashes generally until about fifty years ago, but they have been retained more frequently than elsewhere in Europe on buildings of historic and architectural importance. With the revival of interest in 'primitive' (but durable and economical) paints, I feel that the expertise in these fields which has been maintained in Scandinavia needs to be tapped and investigated. There are other 'primitive' paints still in use there, such as soft distemper, casein (buttermilk) paints and glazes, and the 'falun rott' exterior paint, already mentioned, with which conservationists and painters are more familiar than their counterparts elsewhere. Because of the difficulty of obtaining materials throughout sparsely populated and far from wealthy rural areas, the old rural painters were forced to improvise, to experiment and to make the best use of their available resources.

A 'primitive' paint, like soft distemper, may use the simplest ingredients and yet require intimate knowledge of its characteristics to give the best results. One has only to look at a Swedish painter's recipe book to be struck by the diversity and precision of their tried-and-tested formulae. Where else does the making of soft distemper itemise among other binders, fish glue, hoof and horn glue, rabbit-skin glue and – in the recent books – cellulose or starchy glues like wallpaper paste? And evaluate each result in terms of its 'pearliness', a subtle iridescence which anyone who has experimented with this most lovely, simple and mysteriously satisfying wall-covering will immediately recognise?

Scandinavian experience in these matters is precious, rooted in a still living tradition. If, in a book like this, which attempts to combine the charm of the old ways with the accessibility of the new, we can help to awaken interest in this small corner of special knowledge – small but truly beautiful – both Suzanne and I will feel more than rewarded. And, if what we describe and show makes you want to find out more by visiting the countries concerned, the pleasure will be shared, because they are the least touristy of European countries, full of surprises and, to a painterly eye, rich with interest.

section 3

Small Table

painted midnight blue with stencilled stars

One item of furniture often encountered in Scandinavian homes is the display cupboard (the Norwegians have a special name for it, 'fatehbur') designed to show off the family's finest possessions. Such cupboards may have two or four doors, but what sets them apart from standard pieces are the hinges of the doors, which are designed to open flat on either side. What was displayed would have varied from one household to another, but piles of household linen, often made of home-woven linen, embroidered or edged with tatted lace, were a common sight. In another case, it might have been colourful ceramics, or a collection of pewter dishes and utensils.

The display cupboard shown here is unusual on two counts. Firstly, it stands in an ante-room of Gripsholm Castle (a former royal residence) outside Stockholm, which accounts for the display of gold plate as well as antique pewter. The cupboard itself is unusual in being made of oak, a rare timber in Scandinavia, and its interior is painted with a vivid and memorable design of white stars on a deep blue background, inspired by a night sky.

The paint used would have been the old form of linseed oil paint (see p.154 for the recipe), for both the blue ground and the hand-painted – rather than stencilled – stars. This is a country piece of some antiquity and different in character from most of the furnishings at Gripsholm, which belong to the grander cosmopolitan style favoured by the Scandinavian nobility. But it does not look at all out of place in its baronial setting, and the piquancy of setting out royal regalia in an old rustic 'fatehbur' is indicative of a decorative tradition which frequently mixed the grand with the humble to fresh and charming effect. Another instance of such mixing was the widespread use of checked linen covers on fine antique chairs, or as decorative hangings on a pretty *lit à la Polonaise*.

opposite

Hand-painted stars on a deep blue background make a wonderfully fresh, unexpected decorative treatment for the interior of a massive oak armoire used to display gold plate and pewter in the Swedish castle of Gripsholm, outside Stockholm.

right

The Scandinavian predilection for dressing up simple pieces of furniture with coloured paint and stencils shows to good effect on this modest country side table in two shades of blue.

Step-by-step

Stars are a fashionable decorative theme, and this particular design lends itself easily to anything from entire walls to smaller items of furniture. I thought this would be a quick and pretty way of enlivening a small deal table on camera for a TV spot. Speed here was essential, so the hand-painted stars of the original cupboard design were replaced by stencilled stars, and the slow-drying linseed-oil paint was exchanged for my own fast-drying Paint Magic Woodwash in three colours: Gitane, Midnight and Driftwood. You could substitute a mid-blue matt emulsion for the base coat, plus a deep-blue acrylic paint, like Plaka, for both the deep-blue wash, which brings up the blue base to a subtle depth of colour, and the scatter of off-white (a grey-white made by adding a little raw umber and a dot of black to a white base) stars. Make your own star stencils (see illustration) by tracing off shapes in different sizes on to stencil card through carbon paper. The star shapes should be cut out with a craft knife or scalpel, fitted with a sharp new blade.

The object to be painted should be stripped down to bare wood, sanded smooth, and any cracks, holes or blemishes filled with a proprietary filler and rubbed back flat. Primer or undercoat are not necessary; modern paints bond better with wood when applied directly.

Materials Check-list

- ✦ Mid-blue matt emulsion paint
- ✦ Dark-blue acrylic paint
- ✦ Grey-white acrylic paint
- ✦ 2 in. (5cm) standard brush
- ✦ Round-topped stencil brush
- ✦ Sandpaper or wet-and-dry (fine grade)
- ✦ Stencil card
- ✦ Craft knife
- ✦ Carbon paper
- ✦ Pencil (well sharpened)
- ✦ Tracing paper
- ✦ Matt acrylic varnish
- ✦ Varnishing brush

1

Give the bare wood an all-over coat of the mid-blue Woodwash or matt emulsion. Allow this to dry. A second coat may be needed to achieve the desired opacity. When dry, rub down lightly with sandpaper to smooth out the surfaces. Brush down.

2

Dilute the midnight-blue Plaka or Woodwash in a small bowl with approximately 50 per cent water, stirring to mix. Brush this over a small test area (the back of a table or chair) to check the density of colour and paint. Brush the colour on, then re-brush in the direction of the wood grain beneath. The darker blue should form visible but soft brushmarks. If the brushmarks are too faint, add more colour; if they are lost in the overall dark-blue, add a little more water. Always proceed cautiously at this stage, trying and testing until you are satisfied. The dark-blue should give a translucent stripey effect, with the lighter base colour showing through. Allow the paint to dry. Sand very lightly for smoothness.

3

Decide first how closely you want to position the stencilled stars to each other. The best arrangement will vary, depending on the size and shape of the piece, but aim on the whole for irregular clusters, rather than a regular grid, varying the size of the stars as well as their position.

Spoon a little of the greyish-white star paint on to a saucer or waxed paper plate. Pick some paint up on your stencil brush. Then work off the surplus moisture by 'pouncing' the bristles on to newspaper. Be careful not to overload your brush, otherwise the edges of the star shape will be blurred and tacky. Position the first stencil, using tabs of masking tape to secure it if you feel the need. Then work the bristles round and round through the stencil. The paint dries almost at once. Lift the stencil off. You should have a fine, clear star print. If the print is too faint to register, re-position the stencil and repeat the operation.

4

Carry on dotting in stars over the entire piece. Carrying a star round a sharply angled corner or curve helps give conviction to the design. To achieve this effect, stencil half first, then move the stencil round to complete it, filling in by hand if necessary. Stand back from time to time to get an over-view to make sure that the effect is even.

5

When the piece is quite dry, coat the surfaces with a slightly thinned (one measure of water to nine of varnish) acrylic matt varnish. Allow it to dry. Sand very lightly to smooth, then re-coat. This will give your piece a fair measure of protection without altering the colours or chalky texture. Drawers or doors that 'bind' because the layers of paint and varnish have built up on the surfaces may need some extra sanding until they move freely. Handles and fittings can now be replaced.

N.B. I think this design should look clear and luminous, as shown. But if you feel you would like it to look more 'aged', you can wipe or brush on an 'antiquing' solution.

Tall Cupboard

with 'clouds marbling'

Like 'kurbits' decoration, which it often partnered, the 'clouds marbling' of the northern Swedish province of Hålsingland was an eccentric but gutsy outgrowth of a more sophisticated decorative technique known as 'marmorering', the Swedish term for 'faux marbre'. 'Marmorering' of great skill and verve began to appear on public buildings and great houses during the Baroque period. Real marble is almost non-existent in Sweden so, to create any grand effect, it was natural to turn to a painted imitation, which was also cheaper than importing marble.

'Clouds marbling' belongs to the rustic, provincial painting tradition usually called 'farmer marbling', to distinguish it from the more 'aristocratic' work of experienced professionals, who were often trained abroad. 'Farmer marbling' bears little resemblance to any known stone, but it often achieves, in its primitive way a highly decorative painted effect. Usually, it takes up some aspect of a 'professional' finish, such as zigzags, 'stones' and broken stripes or, in the case of 'clouds marbling', repetitive scallops and develops it into a distinctive and decorative pattern.

One significant difference between courtly 'marmorering' and the country imitation lay in the type of paint used. 'Marmorering' was executed in oil paints and glazes to create the 'softening', transparent, layered effects and other refinements essential to *trompe-l'œil* types of marbling. The country painters, whether from ignorance, thrift, or for speedy execution, often worked in water-based media like distemper, buttermilk (casein-based) glazes, limewash

opposite
This is a truly magnificent example of peasant-style decoration on an old cupboard-cum-bureau, specifically of the stylized, robust form of decoration known in Sweden as 'clouds marbling'.

and so forth. This undoubtedly restricted their work, since water-based media do not permit much subtlety or 'softening' but require a rapid, forceful attack with the brush to create a clear, crude effect. Hence, the wilder examples of 'farmer marbling' can resemble coloured lightning, hugely magnified knitting, strings of sausages or rows of dinosaur eggs!

'Clouds marbling', by comparison, is a touch more sophisticated; it was used on painted furniture in home-made, oil-based paint made from linseed oil thinned with real turpentine. This paint was 'juicy' enough and slow drying enough to be manipulated quite easily. Norwegian 'rosmålning' techniques depend on much the same paint and clearly revel in the freedom the medium brought to their brushwork and glaze-work.

One trick of the trade which the 'clouds' marblers may have adopted from their Norwegian counterparts is the picking up of more than one colour at a time on the brush, so that the strokes are doubled up or hemmed with a contrasting tint. Thus the scallops which make up the 'pattern' of 'clouds marbling' might be composed of strokes three-quarters dark blue and the last quarter near-white. The result of the brush being taken through a typical arc would be a dark, thundery-blue centre with a pale outer rim. Achieving such an effect must have needed patience in the choice of suitable colours and the proper width of brush and the laying out of colours on the palette. The gain would have been in time and a certain coherence in the painting, but for many rustic craftsmen it might have seemed easier to work in the dark, thunder-blue scallops and then whisk round these with a slender, whippy brush, like the 'sword-liner', a favourite of Scandinavian painters. This brush takes some getting used to, but it can become a painter's pet once its potential is realized.

Step-by-step

It really does seem to be the case that, with Nordic decoration, the further north you go, the more imaginative and, sometimes, bizarre will be the products of the local craftsmen. With less exposure to fashionable trends and artefacts, such local painters often developed highly idiosyncratic and individual styles, usually in the context of workshops specializing in producing vivid painted pieces for sale on commission or in markets and fairs. The 'clouds marbling' technique of Hålsingland is just such a development, a folk creation incorporating bold swirling arabesques of colour with a remote resemblance to marble, but with a vigorous and highly decorative quality of its own. Since it was usually executed in tones of blue, from thundercloud to cirrhus white, the name, 'clouds marbling', is self-explanatory. Usually it is used to create a strong contrast to the red oxide known as 'English red'. Sometimes, however, the 'clouds marbling' is used simply as a frame to a wonderfully bold and vigorous floral panel on a door or cupboard. Like so many folk techniques, it is literally a hands-on activity, using thumbs and fingers as well as brushes.

The technique is shown here applied to an old, but not specially Scandinavian, pine cupboard; it has a massive cornice, tall boxy shape and lightly arched panel on the door. The painting was done throughout with water-based acrylic emulsion paints plus Flow Enhancer and scumble. The finishing, however, is done in oil-based varnish for durability and a touch of 'fattiness' which lean water paints sometimes seem to lack.

Materials Check-list

- ✦ White matt emulsion tinted with Prussian blue, plus tiny amounts of black and ochre for base coat
- ✦ Raw umber
- ✦ Fat fitch or 2in. (5cm) brush
- ✦ Finer fitch or fat water-colour brush
- ✦ Barn Red Woodwash
- ✦ Liquitex Flow Enhancer
- ✦ Either Craig and Rose Extra Pale Dead Flat *or* Matt Acrylic Varnish
- ✦ Fine sandpaper

1

The entire cupboard, cleaned of any grease or wax with white spirit and wire wool, is base painted with a light, slightly grey, sky-blue. Two coats are needed for cover, which are sanded down between coats to smooth, but not back to the wood in this case.

2

Over the dry pale blue, a
medium-tone blue (a little raw
umber is added, plus more
Prussian blue, to the original mix)
is brushed in bold scallops as
shown, using a fat fitch or 2 in.
(5cm) brush. Make these quite
wide, 3-4 in. (7.5-10cm), in a
double row. Smooth out with
thumbs or fingers.

3

Mix a deep, thundery blue-black,
adding more blue, a little black
and a touch more raw umber.
Brush this on the leading edge of
the scallop shapes, smoothing
back into the colour already
applied with thumbs, fingers or
a clean brush.

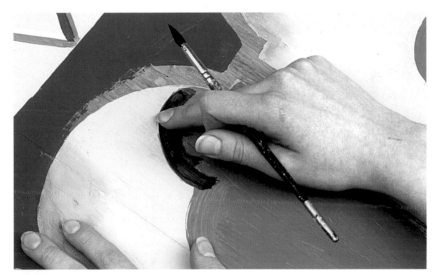

4

These thunder clouds are
dramatized by a pale – if not
silver – lining. Use a finer fitch or
fat watercolour brush to apply the
grey-white emulsion mixed with
Flow Enhancer to lighten the
outer rim of the dark thundery
scallops. Soften these pale shapes
by smudging slightly with thumbs
or brush.

5

Add bold red-brown touches. We used a Barn Red Woodwash, but other brown-red acrylic shades could be used – Venetian red, Indian red, etc. Pick out the mouldings, add 'faux' details, outline the drawers, etc.

6

Stand back at this point and give your piece a critical once-over. It may need darkening in some spots, more highlighting in others. You may want to add more red detail. Another possible feature, shown on our Hålsingland piece, is the addition of almost random squiggles and trefoil spots in black, to run counter to the movement of the burgeoning cloud shapes. Here and there is a slight suggestion that the black scribble is imitating veining.

7

Varnish the piece well: it could be a future heirloom. I suggest three coats of either Craig and Rose Extra Pale Dead Flat or Matt Acrylic Varnish. Rub down carefully between each coat. If you want to soften and 'antique' the colours, do this after the first coat of varnish, using a wash of raw umber rubbed on with a soft rag. Then re-varnish.

Woven Birch Bark Baskets

'stamped' with carved cork

Basket-making as a craft seems to have evolved rather late in Scandinavia, not contributing significantly to the peasant economy until the late eighteenth century. It is said that the craft had had depressing connotations previously, being associated with piece-work in the poorhouse. However, an indiginous Swedish form of basket-weaving appeared in Dalarna towards the end of the eighteenth century and had such success that basket vendors piled their sleighs high and travelled as far abroad as St. Petersburg to sell the products of their long winter.

In Finland baskets were woven from roots, and resembled a wilder and knottier form of macramé. The Swedes used long strips of spruce, birch and other softwoods, ingeniously prepared by separating the inner rings of a tree's growth and splitting them longitudinally. Arranged like a many-pointed star, these provided the skeleton of the 'korg' or basket. The base was woven first, then the flexible strips were bent up and the sides shaped and formed by diagonal interweaving. Scraps of the outer bark and heart-wood, peeled smooth and shaped with sharp knives and simple traditional tools, made the firm upper rim and the handles, which were sturdily riveted to the basic form. These baskets were made to suit a variety of needs – baby baskets, school lunch baskets, knap-sacks, 'berry baskets', shallow trugs for cut logs and many other forms. Being light, strong and simple, they shared in their raw state many of the virtues of traditional basketry, a craft dating back to prehistoric times. It was inevitable, however, given their invitingly smooth latticed surfaces and the unique decorative impulses of Nordic peasant culture which was in a

opposite

This old photograph brings to life the real history of the trades and crafts of the Nordic countries.

class of its own, that 'korg' and paint, used creatively and exuberantly, would soon meet. It was not long before these baskets acquired their own distinctive decorative treatments, usually exploiting the lattice construction in a simple but satisfying way. The coloured chequerboard that resulted was often given a speedy but effective decorative flourish by means of carved stamps, which made the baskets individual, charming and economical to produce. The closest in spirit to these delightful but ephemeral products, perhaps, might be the papered hat and bonnet boxes which are one of the most appealing legacies of early nineteenth-century American retail trade. Such modest household items were made quickly and sold cheaply, but a great many old examples have survived, adding their own light-hearted prettiness to a culture where most artefacts were still made to last and hence demanded more 'serious' treatment.

An early photograph shows a young and hand-some woman, dressed in an embroidered sheepskin coat and flowing skirt, about to set off with her sleigh piled high with baskets painstakingly made in the long dark days leading up to Christmas. These would have been made by a family enterprise as second string to the usual seasonal trades of fishing, forestry and agriculture. The money from the sale of the baskets must have helped to keep many Swedish rural families going during the months before the weather would allow them to resume their habitual trades. This unknown young woman, with a swagger that suggests she can handle tough bargaining, about to launch herself into the snow-bound Swedish winter to sell her family's winter work, epitomizes the down-to-earth courage which must have sustained her race through centuries of hard graft, a tough pride that dealt wth inflexible realities with guts and courage but also with indomitable grace and style.

Step-by-step

Peasant societies waste nothing, and those of the Scandinavian countries are no exception. These countries are rich in silver birches, prized for their wood. The bark is removed and the exposed wood is shaved off in fine strips and woven in a simple lattice to make baskets of all shapes and sizes, from sturdy rucksacks to tiny baskets just big enough to hold a bunch of flowers or a present for a child. It is customary to decorate the baskets in a chequer-board design of two or more colours and then stamp these coloured squares with home-made decorative stamps carved from whatever material is to hand, usually cork. Champagne corks make excellent stamps, being large and made from higher-grade cork. Rubber door stops can also be adapted to make stamps, as Suzanne found. Use a craft knife or scalpel for carving, keep the design simple, and watch your fingers! The design does not have to be deeply cut (1/5 in. [5mm] is enough as a rule) but test the stamp on paper to check the impression. The same stamps can be used on other surfaces, of course, such as flower-pots, boxes, trays and so on.

Materials Check-list

◆ Corks, door-stops
◆ Swan scalpel with extra blades
◆ Felt-tip pen
◆ Match-pot sizes of matt emulsion or acrylic colours in several shades, including raw umber
◆ Flat-ended brush, approximately 1/2 in. (1.5cm), preferably hog's bristle
◆ Standard decorating brush for 'antiquing'
◆ Saucers or pot lids
◆ Newspaper
◆ Tissues
◆ Matt acrylic varnish

1

Draw the design on the cork first – it is surprising how even the simplest daisy-flower motif can drop a petal if you don't rough it out beforehand. The cork is then carved with a scalpel fitted with a new blade. Clear the background away by whittling carefully.

2

*The basket is painted in a deep-blue acrylic paint on
alternate squares, using a soft-bristle, flat brush, and
the rim is coloured to match.*

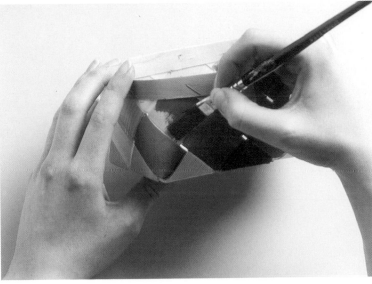

3

*Remaining squares in this
example are coloured in with a
mulberry acrylic paint.*

4

A four-leaf clover stamp, dipped in standard white emulsion and 'pounced' lightly on to paper, is pressed on to the mulberry squares.

5

The whole basket is washed over with an 'antiquing' mixture of raw umber and a spot of black diluted in water. This softens and blends strong colour contrasts. Varnish if you wish with matt acrylic varnish.

Oval Box

in the Gustavian style

Wooden boxes, in all shapes and sizes, were important items for storage in Scandinavian rural homes. Where people lived so closely together, it must have been very important to keep one's prized possessions apart in an identifiable box marked with the owner's initials. The man of the house, for instance, would keep his shaving tackle in a distinctive box, long and narrow with a chip-carved lid. The womenfolk were in charge of the 'church box', which held the family prayer book and was taken to church on Sunday. Festive headgear, wonderfully elaborate crowns and be-ribboned head-dresses in the style of the region, were stored in large round boxes. Even children had their individual 'barnaskorna' in southern Sweden, in which they kept their personal treasures.

Oval or round boxes like the one used in our project were light and portable; they were traditionally made of fine strips or shavings of birch, beech or fir, flexible enough to bend into the desired shape and fastened to a base, with the overlapping ends stitched in place with birch roots. They were used for all sorts of purposes: for instance, as storage for needles and thread, trinkets or ribbons.

As was usual with small objects, the boxes were decorated to make them more personal and give them individuality. In the case of the betrothal boxes which are such a charming relic of more ceremonious times, the decoration was intended to honour and flatter the recipient and, at the same time, properly symbolize the intention and feelings of the giver. A young man would present his betrothed with a special box, often richly decorated, inscribed with her initials and the date. Sometimes these boxes were made by the young man himself, sometimes a professional painter was employed, but invariably the box contained an assortment of little gifts made or chosen by the bridegroom to be. These might be trinkets, ribbons or perhaps a carved spoon. In it, the bride to be would keep any letters from her fiancé, perhaps a 'likeness' or dried flowers: in other words, all the sentimental bits and pieces which a young woman would collect and treasure during the time between her betrothal and her wedding day.

In earlier centuries the 'svepta' boxes were decorated with carved or burned-in patterns, but in the eighteenth century such traditional styles of decoration, which went back to the time of the Vikings, went out of fashion in the face of a taste for bright and fanciful painted styles. The favourite was Rococo and the favoured background colour was blue. The decorative elements might be in any colour, though red and white were always popular. Much play was made of the initials of the betrothed, the date, and sometimes a motto or proverb were added.

opposite
Traditional Norwegian 'rosmålning' makes a handsome object of this sturdy old wooden oval box with a snugly fitting lid and solid handle.

right
The crudeness of this oval box, both in its making and its decoration, suggest that it is a genuinely home-made piece.

Step-by-step

This is an excellent example of how the most casual, impressionistic effects and the most primitive equipment – fingers as well as brushes – can produce a decorative effect which is both elegant and truly authentic in what one might call 'country-meets-Gustavian' style. The oval box was painted entirely with water-based acrylics and a little white emulsion. Some of the pretty wood base is left showing, adding to the transparent, clouded effect.

Materials Check-list

- ✦ Sandpaper
- ✦ Standard white emulsion
- ✦ Pthalo blue, lamp-black and white acrylic for mid blue
- ✦ Raw and burnt umber for 'dirtying'
- ✦ Standard paint brush
- ✦ Selection of fine sable brushes for decorative detail
- ✦ Craig and Rose Extra Pale Dead Flat Varnish

1

Oval shapes are first suggested with white, progressing round the sides of the box. These are immediately filled with a pale grey-blue, leaving a white rim to one side, and bare wood in between. Smudge the two colours together slightly with your fingers.

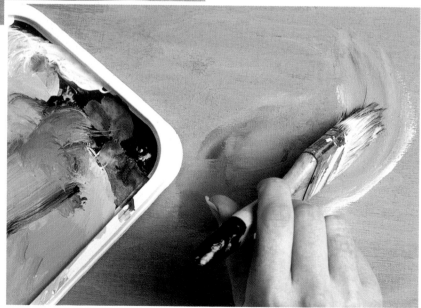

2

A wavering line in a 'dirty' shade of greeny-brown (burnt umber with a hint of raw umber) is drawn round each ellipse and then again smudged firmly with the fingers and thumb, drawing the darker colour back across the grey-blue shapes.

3

Using all the same colours but a finer brush, the oval box lid is then wreathed in delicate scrollwork and centred with a pretty and elegant motif. This is worked as before, with white first, then mid-blue, leaving some white, then slightly darker lines (not smudged here, but slightly softened with the brush) then dark details and white highlights are added with a fine sable brush. When dry, the whole box is finished with a protective coat of Craig and Rose Extra Pale Dead Flat Varnish.

Bentwood Chairs

with Scandinavian-inspired 'distressed' finish

Scandinavian furniture painting was invariably done to a high standard, using many thin coats of paint rubbed back to give a smooth, durable surface. There are, however, inevitably examples of old domestic pieces like the dresser shown here, which have been so much handled over the years that the original finish has been abraded or eroded, so that the next layer down – in this case the bare pine itself – shows through to a greater or lesser extent. Such are the scars of time and use. A decade ago, or even less, such pieces would almost certainly have been stripped, waxed and sold (by a dealer, anyway) as old stripped pine.

I well remember a piece of old furniture being offered for sale as 'stripped pine'. With hindsight, it occurs to me that it was originally a painted piece in the eighteenth-century Swedish style, which had been 'cleaned up' by an owner or dealer. Nowadays, however, it would be considered wanton folly to dunk an old painted piece in a stripping tank, because the original paint finish, however scarred and shabby, is now accepted by the more discerning dealers and collectors at least as a valuable record of a piece's history and provenance. Stripped pine of whatever age is much of a muchness; old painted pine is indi-

vidual and authentic. Its worn coats of colour tell a story we want to hear.

Obviously, you need to be able to spot the difference between the 'real' original painted finish and any later smartening-up operations. If the piece looks interesting, however worn in its present state, my advice would be to leave it as it is. If a crude, inappropriate coat of gloss enamel seems to conceal a finer original finish (scrape a less visible part to check), there may be a case for attempting to resurrect the original, older paint finish. The only safe way to do this, sadly and laboriously, is to chip off the surface coat, using a strong, not-too-sharp instrument, such as a small screwdriver or shave hook. Serious antique dealers are sometimes driven to such measures. I remember watching a young Swedish girl working away on an old painted chair, flake by flake, in the window of an antique shop in Stockholm's old town. Her incentive was the knowledge that the chair would be worth twice as much in its original covering.

Such a 'distressed' paint finish can be recreated and the look and 'feel' of an old, worn painted softwood piece can be quickly and readily given to a new or new-ish piece, using state-of-the-art paints and a few simple tricks.

opposite
The simple, rectilinear construction, wooden seat and bright paint finish all proclaim this as an essentially peasant piece. The 'kurbits' motif painted on the wall behind confirms that this is a well-to-do peasant home in the Swedish province of Dalarna.

left
A trio of bentwood chairs have been given an unmistakably Scandinavian air with a pale painted finish and an ingenious fake 'caned' effect on the seats, using a buttermilk glaze patterned with home-made combs to imitate cane.

Step-by-step

The guinea-pigs shown here are a pair of standard bentwood chairs with caned seats, which I picked up for a song in a back street junk shop. The caning was covered by plush, which had been stapled to the frame, while the bentwood had been finished crudely in gold paint. I liked the idea of applying a 'distressed' finish to the chairs because, though not traditional to bentwood, I thought it would bring the curvy outlines to life in a contemporary way. The same approach works equally well on what joiners call 'new-built' carpentry, such as kitchen fittings consisting partly of timber, partly of MDF (medium density fibreboard), or fitted cupboards in bedrooms, bathrooms, etc., made from a medley of materials which have little appeal if left unadorned. The 'distressed' effect described here adds texture as well as colour, a suggestion of age and use which is attractive in itself. If you key the two colours involved to your room colours, you have the added advantage that the results are almost guaranteed to fit in with their surroundings.

Materials Check-list

✦ Fine surface filler
✦ Woodwash (or matt emulsion) in contrasting shades (here yellow ochre and mulberry)
✦ Standard household wax candle
✦ Pads of medium and fine-grade wire wool
✦ Matt varnish
✦ Standard paint brushes

1

The plush seats were first removed by levering up the staples with a sharp screwdriver. The staple holes were filled with fine surface filler and sanded back till smooth. The bentwood frames were also sanded to smooth out the gold paint finish, though not back to the bare wood.

2

Surfaces for these distressing techniques must be as near clean and bare as possible. Old paint, rubbed down to create a 'key' for subsequent coats, is a feasible base; spray-on lacquer, the standard factory finish, is too hard and non-porous to bond properly with water-based acrylic-type paints, unless the surface is thoroughly rubbed down and roughened. New-built surfaces, such as MDF (medium density fibreboard) need different preparation; one or two coats of a fast-drying shellac or spirit-based varnish (button polish) will do the trick, sealing the porous surface so that the water content does not seep in and warp the boards. All holes, cracks, etc. should be filled (unless you feel they might add to the final effect) with fine surface filler. Allow to dry, then sand back till smooth and level. Stop out with shellac.

3

Apply a solid opaque coat of your first base colour over the entire surface. When choosing colour combinations for 'distressing' you should obviously be guided by existing colours in your room, but it is worth knowing that strong contrasts (e.g. yellow and blue) look bold and feisty, whereas softer harmonies (e.g. pink and grey-green, dull blue and cream) will result in a gentle overall effect to which the layering of colours adds warmth and character. The top coat of colour will predominate, so this is the one that needs to match your room scheme. Apply your chosen base paint evenly over the entire surface, using a standard brush. If it dries patchily, re-coat to give an opaque colour. Smooth lightly with wire wool and dust down.

N.B. If you are working on old pine and want this to act as base colour omit all these preliminaries.

4

Use the wax candle, held like a pencil, or rubbed on its side, to place a thick layer of wax over your piece wherever you want the undercolour to show through. On the bentwood chairs, I used the 'distressing' to emphasize the curves of the seats and backs. On a piece to which you want to give an instant 'antique' look, use the wax mainly on areas of wear, round knobs and handles, cupboard-door fronts, on the leading edge of shelves or counter tops. Don't skimp on wax – too much is better than too little. For a fairly even overall distressing effect, apply the candle sideways to give a pleasant speckled finish. On base wood use the candle in just the same way, as a 'parting agent'.

5

Re-paint the whole piece, using the chosen top colour and covering over both the undercolour and waxing with a standard brush. Again the colour should be opaque, for contrast. Allow the piece to dry thoroughly.

6

Wearing gloves, take up a generous handful of medium grade wire wool and rub this firmly in the direction of the grain of the piece, or where the grain would be in the case of MDF. You will see the colour beneath breaking through cleanly and attractively almost at once. Continue over the whole piece, taking care not to rub so hard that you go through both paint layers.

Some emulsion paints take a 'burnish' if you go over the surface with a finer grade wire wool and a fine polish. If the piece is going to take a lot of wear, it is a good idea to give it one or two coats of matt or eggshell varnish. When this is quite hard, rub down lightly with wire wool to smooth the surface, then dust down. A light coat of dark-tan shoe-polish can be applied over the varnish with a soft cloth and buffed up to 'antique' the colours and bring up a terrific shine.

Norwegian Clock

with rustic Rococo design

Many years ago, when I lived by the sea in Dorset, a highly unusual longcase clock appeared in the window of a local antique shop. The shape immediately caught my eye. Compared to the traditional English longcase, or 'grandfather clock', tall and straight, with the pendulum swinging behind a glazed window, this was a decidedly curvaceous piece, with a round moon face above a case which swelled below with something of the grace of a violin. The case was of pine – good quality, but almost certainly stripped in recent years. The clock's other feature was an astonishing alarm, which the dealer demonstrated for me; it went off with the shrill urgency of a fire engine's bell. I had never seen a clock like it and I coveted it greatly. Sadly, by the time money arrived which would have allowed me to buy it, the clock had gone.

It is always the extravagances one resisted that continue to haunt one. I can still visualize that clock clearly, especially now that I know that it was almost certainly a 'Mora-klocka', the most prized status symbol among the more prosperous Swedish peasantry during the late eighteenth and early nineteenth centuries. Judging by examples I subsequently saw in Sweden, it would have originally been quite lavishly decorated with stylized bouquets in the Dalarna style, since Mora, where the mechanisms of these clocks were made, was a town in that central Swedish province.

The possession of a 'Mora-klocka' was a sign that a peasant household was prospering and such a clock would enjoy pride of place in the home. Sometimes, to make it even more conspicuous, the long-case clock was built into the side or foot of a cupboard bed, giving it a commanding position in the room and, presumably, keeping the bed's occupants awake with its chimes. Certainly, with an alarm as fiendishly efficient as the one I heard, there would have been little risk of sleeping through it.

Not all Scandinavian clocks were in the Rococo style described here. There were 'Mora-klocka' which were almost indistinguishable from the European 'grandfathers' in shape and proportions, except that the former were gaudy with floral decoration, or 'kurbits' motifs, or had their carved areas picked out in colour. Perhaps the most disarming of all the distinctive regional clocks is the one known as the 'Bride of Angermanland', where the female curves of the Rococo style have been exaggerated to portray a bride of this far-northern province in her wedding finery, from bridal crown to bridal belt with hanging purse, all carved in relief and picked out in characteristic colours – red, white, yellow and green. Richly colourful and oddly anthropomorphic, these splendid 'bride' clocks represent Swedish peasant culture at its most exuberant.

opposite
A highly decorated 'Mora' clock has pride of place in this colourful Swedish interior. Note the spoon rack on the 'kurbits' decorated wall.

right
A curvaceous longcase clock can be glimpsed through a doorway. This is an aristocratic house and the clock is therefore conventional in decoration.

Step-by-step

The original of the design shown here was on a much larger scale, spread over the vivid blue walls of a wooden house in Norway. I was looking for a pretty design to dress up the face – or façade – of a quaint pedimented clock in MDF (medium density fibreboard) and the pink roses on a blue ground looked right. This is another of those designs where frivolous scrolls and flicks of white imposed on smudges of pink and dark blue really create the design. As with Norwegian 'rosmålning', everything is in the brushwork, and the freer and more confident this is – practice makes perfect, undoubtedly – the more authentic and charming your efforts will look.

The clock was painted entirely with fast-drying acrylics, but with the addition of Liquitex Flow Enhancer to improve 'flow' and help the correction of any careless flourish. Without this, acrylics are stodgy and lack the flexibility of oils. But – and this is a big but – they dry so much more quickly that a design like this can be completed in a session, an impossibility with oils.

1

After two coats of shellac, sanded back, to seal and smooth the MDF (otherwise this material is too porous) the clock front gets an all-over coat of a vivid sky-blue, made from pthalo blue acrylic mixed into a little white emulsion.

Materials Check-list

- ✦ Shellac, sandpaper and methylated spirit as usual for sealing and smoothing
- ✦ Pthalo blue acrylic/ white emulsion
- ✦ Burnt sienna or Venetian red acrylic
- ✦ Midnight Woodwash (for deep blue) plus lamp-black gouache
- ✦ Liquitex Flow Enhancer
- ✦ 1 in. (2.5cm) standard brush or 1 in. (2.5cm) glider for applying base coats
- ✦ Selection of sable brushes for decoration, including a longer haired brush (Pro Arte no. 4) for longer tendrils, etc.
- ✦ Raw and burnt umber (acrylics or powder colours)
- ✦ Gum arabic
- ✦ Craig and Rose Eggshell Varnish
- ✦ Rottenstone powder
- ✦ Rags
- ✦ Saucers for mixing
- ✦ Paper to practise strokes

2
Red acrylic half-mixed with white is then dabbed on and smudged with the fingers to make rosy-to-white blobs. These are the foundation for the roses and buds.

3
Deep blue tendrils, blobs and leaf shapes are then put in to make two curving arms that will encircle the paper clock-face. This will be added, pasted and sealed with gum arabic last of all.

4
White tendrils, scrolls, flicks and dots have been superimposed on the pink and blue shapes to suggest roses, buds, fronds and other graceful shapes. These all work together to suggest an asymmetric wreath, the mark of Rococo decoration. The white shapes are strengthened here by underlining with blue-black. This is made by adding a spot of lamp-black gouache to the previous blue-black mixture. At this stage the design is established, but it is still a little crude.

5

Some bold, though quite unrealistic, marbling on the pediment seemed appropriate to the colour scheme and the general architectural air of this clock. The base is marbled likewise. All the same colours (bar the pink) which have been used previously are incorporated in the marbling: deep blue and blue-black 'splodged' across the mouldings, with white veins 'twiddled' on with a fine brush as shown. Any softening or smudging is done with the fingers.

6

A 'dirty' antiquing glaze – raw and burnt umber in a little Flow Enhancer – is brushed over the entire clock, then wiped back to leave just a tinge, giving a greeny tint to the blue and helping to unify all the elements in the decoration.

7

The paper clock-face (a photo-copy) is sealed and glued in place with gum arabic, a traditional adhesive that does not discolour or transparentize the paper. Then the entire clock is given a coat of Craig and Rose Eggshell Varnish, rubbed back with a rottenstone paste to kill the shine slightly.

Corner Cupboard

with birch graining

The idea of dressing up a piece of cheap wooden furniture with special paint effects to make it look more expensive is not new. Ability in graining, as a technical qualification for a decorative painter, traditionally ranked alongside skill in marbling as a mark of achievement; indeed the same painter was usually adept at both techniques. The fashion for grained surfaces, imitating wood with paint or glazes by means of special tools with picturesque names (floggers, draggers, rockers, etc.) seems historically to have followed close on the heels of the eighteenth-century fashion for exotic hardwoods or rare veneers. This created an appetite for similar status symbols in the homes of the less affluent. The most frequently encountered variant of graining in Scandinavia was mahogany imitation, which proliferated in the early nineteenth century after the adoption of the original wood by the leading English and French furniture makers of the preceding century. There seems to have been scarcely a home of the period, from comfortable town house to primitive peasant cottage, which did not display the aspirations of its occupants through local softwood pieces grained to resemble, often quite implausibly, the strong red-brown or tawny colouring and bold markings of a fine cut of African or Cuban mahogany.

Both the grained pieces themselves and the standard of graining skills employed varied wildly. The furniture included substantial and finely made Baltic secretaires and immense Biedermeier-style sofas which occupied pride of place in bourgeois villas. Such pieces were grained skilfully by professional painters using sophisticated tools, oil paints and transparent glazes. In contrast, there were the sturdy but crude chests of drawers owned by peasant families; invariably made from pine, they tended to exhibit the bizarre effects resulting from scant acquaintance with the timber in question and the use of home-made glazes based on vinegar, stale beer and buttermilk, which were applied with such rudimentary tools as hands and thumbs, rags, 'combs' made from notched cardboard, corks and string.

Such rustic graining, while a long way from being a faithful facsimile of the original timber, has a vigour and brio all its own. The stylized patterns, which developed and were endlessly copied, form a whole sub-section of the 'folk' decoration of the time.

Rather than imitate the Scandinavian grainers' imitation of a foreign wood, we thought it would be more interesting for this graining project to concentrate on a less familiar, but typically Scandinavian timber, birch. It has the pale golden tone popularized in Biedermeier furniture in the first half of the nineteenth century, often enlivened by the local grainer's addition of dark, formalized squiggles. Used simply, as here, this makes an intriguing finish for a little set of corner shelves of the sort often found in Scandinavian peasant homes and used to display anything from the paterfamilias' pipes and tobacco jar, to the husfru's cherished china ornaments, often Staffordshire, brought home by a sailor son. In another context, combined with mahogany graining for richness, ebony banding or 'picking out' adds a certain chic to the piece. Instead of homely buttermilk, beer or vinegar, the medium used here is entirely state-of-the-art acrylic, both for speed and easy handling.

opposite

A splendid, sophisticated example of oak graining on a wooden door shows just how expert Scandinavian graining can be. Very little oak timber survives in northern Scandinavia, so oak graining would have a special status appeal.

Step-by-step

Birch graining is not often seen outside Scandinavia, but it makes an attractive blond finish enlivened with little dark squiggles. It goes well, for instance, on a Biedermeier-style grained piece, contrasting effectively with rich mahogany and dark ebony. It is not difficult to do, but applying the squiggles requires patience. Our example was executed entirely in water-based paint as far as the final varnish.

Materials Check-list

- ✦ 500ml button polish with glider for application
- ✦ Methylated spirit for brush cleaning
- ✦ Standard white emulsion
- ✦ Ochre and burnt umber powder pigment
- ✦ Liquitex Flow Enhancer
- ✦ Raw sienna powder pigment or acrylic tube colour
- ✦ Lamp-black gouache
- ✦ Two watercolour brushes, one 2 in. (5cm) for the 'contour maps', one no. 8 Prolene Pro Arte for the squiggles
- ✦ Craig and Rose Eggshell Varnish
- ✦ Fine sandpaper
- ✦ Fine wire wool

1

After the routine application of shellac and sanding to seal the wood, the corner cupboard was painted all over with a creamy, buff-coloured paint by mixing a little ochre and burnt umber powder pigment dissolved in water into standard white emulsion. Don't mix too much for a piece this size – a teacupful is plenty. Re-coat when dry if the base coat looks patchy.

2

Using a medium-sized watercolour brush (no.8) and an amber-tinted solution of Liquitex Flow Enhancer coloured with raw sienna and a tinge of burnt umber acrylic tube colours, brush in 'contour maps' as shown over the entire piece. Start with the central 'ring' or ellipse, then brush in further rings moving outwards. Fill in intervals with parallel loops or 'hillocks'.

3

Seal this graining in with one coat of button polish diluted with a splash of methylated spirit. Brush over evenly.

4

Use a fine sable brush with a little brown-black glaze (mix burnt umber and black gouache into some Flow Enhancer) to add little dark squiggles and an occasional dot over the whole piece, spaced fairly evenly as shown. Allow the piece to dry.

Chest
with vinegar graining

The art of graining – using paint and glazes to simulate wood grain – was especially widely practised during the nineteenth century when the fashion for hardwood furniture, representative of bourgeois solidity and affluence, seems to have reached its height. Those who could not afford the real thing, which would have meant all but the most prosperous peasants in rural Scandinavia, opted for a 'grained' imitation; of the hardwoods imitated, mahogany was the most popular.

It would be a mistake to suppose that Scandinavian graining was always rustic in character. There are excellent examples of highly sophisticated graining to be found in old public buildings, banks, churches and other institutions. Whereas the skilled practitioner aimed for verisimilitude, however, the self-taught country painters tended to go for bold effects, partly because no doubt they lacked models to copy and partly, too, because their clients found this style more impressive as well as affordable. Speed of execution was another consideration when negotiating a commission with thrifty peasants.

It is hardly surprising, then, that rustic graining tended to be executed in simple home-made media which were relatively easy to handle and which allowed stylish effects to be achieved rapidly. Instead of the complex layering of oil and water glazes, softened by expensive brushes, combs and other tools, which were the stock-in-trade of his city counterparts, the journeyman painter usually settled for one coat of a dark brown-black glaze, based on vinegar, flat ale, beer or buttermilk, which was brushed over a base of iron-oxide red or yellow ochre, depending on the tone of wood required, and then quickly mottled, streaked and swirled with whatever tools came to hand. These could include fingertips, the side of the palm, a chamois leather, combs cut from card, corks and so on.

These thin, highly pigmented glazes are exceptionally easy to manipulate, encouraging a bold, impressionistic style of 'wood imitation', as graining is called in Scandinavia. Anyone who has experimented with these old media will understand how it came about that mahogany imitation was characterised by such bizarre effects as feral spots and stripes, swooping arabesques, squiggles and pot-hooks. A lump of putty, used like a stamp or rolled over the surface of the wet glaze, produces a captivating variety of marks, with the added bonus of incidental 'sea-weed' shapes which seem to be created by a reaction between the linseed oil in the putty and the vinegar in the glaze. All these fluid – as distinct from oily – glazes, dry completely matt. In this state they look dull, like dry pebbles. A coat or two of semi-shiny varnish, however, will make them spring to life as vividly as the same pebbles under water. One or two protective coats of varnish are absolutely necessary with glazes like these; otherwise they would simply wash off again. The original varnishes of many nineteenth century pieces have now worn away to some extent, so the effect is not as shiny-smart as when they were originally applied. But the exuberance of their decoration undeniably remains an object lesson in making the best of the simplest of techniques and materials.

Modern decorators might like to note that the same primitive techniques can look quite different with a simple change of colour scheme. A deep blue vinegar glaze over pale green, for instance, can give excitingly different results with the same simple technique.

opposite
This sturdy old chest of drawers is very typical of the graining techniques in use in the nineteenth century, largely executed with ad-hoc tools.

Step-by-step

The small chest shown is the sort of piece that can still be picked up for next to nothing. Mine was in good enough condition to work on immediately and I thought it would be fun to see how far it could be upgraded by that favourite technique of the nineteenth-century country furniture-maker, vinegar graining. Sometimes, stale beer was used instead of vinegar. A dark-brown glaze on a yellow base simulated walnut, while a dark brown-black glaze over red oxide was a favourite way of imitating mahogany; examples of this can be seen all over Scandinavia. It is a technique to have fun with, quick and absurdly simple but undoubtedly effective. I added the contrasting painted trim, because I thought the plainness of the piece could do with a little light relief. This finish looks great on pine blanket-boxes, hanging shelves, deed boxes and even tin trunks. Clean all pieces well, then base paint with the same red oxide metal primer, a cheap, useful paint which happens to be just the right colour.

Materials Check-list

✦ 1 litre red oxide metal primer
✦ White spirit
✦ Standard 2 in. (5cm) paint-brush, plus smaller brush for corners
✦ Small bottle malt vinegar or ½ pint flat beer
✦ 1 oz. burnt umber dry pigment
✦ Lamp-black gouache (optional)
✦ Lump linseed-oil putty
✦ Assorted implements: cork, corn-cob, rags, etc.
✦ Sandpaper
✦ Shellac mixture (50 per cent white polish, 50 per cent button polish)
✦ 2 in. (5cm) glider
✦ Methylated spirit to clean glider
✦ Acrylic colours for final ornamentation (optional)
✦ Craig and Rose Eggshell Varnish or equivalent
✦ Rottenstone

1
The small chest is base-coated with iron oxide metal primer.

2

*When dry it is lightly rubbed back
with find sandpaper and then a
second coat is applied.*

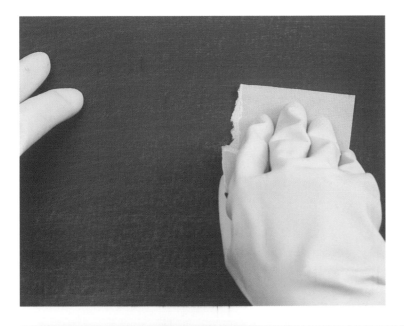

3

*Mix a fluid glaze of approximately
1/2 pint malt vinegar (or flat beer) to
which you add 2-3 tablespoons of burnt
umber powder pigment, mixing
thoroughly. Test the colour and
consistency on a corner of the piece – it
will wipe off easily with a damp rag.
The colour should be dark-brown and
brush out smoothly without 'cissing' –
bubbling up. If this happens, re-brushing
backwards and forwards usually solves
the problem. A tiny squirt of washing-up
liquid can also be a help. Brush glaze
over one surface of the piece at a time.*

4

All sorts of ad hoc implements can be used to manipulate this readily malleable glaze, from one's thumb, to the side of the hand (popular with Swedes and Danes – shown left), to lumps of putty rolled until soft and pressed on to the surface (right), or dried corn-cobs rolled to make fan shapes at the corners. Play around until you find an arrangement that suits your piece; how much it resembles mahogany grain or feathering or how much it is purely a fun finish is entirely up to you. Any wrong moves can be wiped off again with a damp sponge.

5

Having decided on a suitable arrangement of shapes, glaze and grain the piece, one side at a time. It is probably best to dry each side with a hair-dryer before moving on. Putty may well create interesting little seaweedy shapes by the reaction of the linseed oil it contains to the vinegar. When the piece is complete and dry, apply two coats of shellac (50/50 button polish and white polish) which will bring up the graining like water on a pebble and provide a smooth base for any further lining, bands or stencilling in gold powders. These were more commonly used on American grained country furniture (e.g. Hitchcock chairs) than on their Scandinavian counterparts.

6

Finish, for strength and durability, with two coats of Craig and Rose Eggshell Varnish or a similar polyurethane varnish. For a super smooth finish, rub round and round over the final varnish coat with a rottenstone paste applied with a rag then wiped off.

Drop-leaf Dining Table

with Gustavian decoration

The idea of a table with fold-out flaps, which took up next to no space in the closed position but extended to a generous size when opened out, was guaranteed success in Scandinavian rural homes, where space was limited and there was a tradition of dual-purpose pieces. Tables of this sort could and can be seen in homes ranging from the simplest log cabin to the 'bondagård' or modest country house. The design and finish of the tables tends to vary accordingly: the peasant version being chunky and heavy looking, with squared-off leaves, undecorated, while the upmarket version is much more graceful, the flaps usually rounded or oval, the legs more slender, and the whole piece painted in one of the pale Gustavian shades, with or without applied decoration. Much thought went into planning the painted decoration, so that the table would still look elegant when folded down and positioned against a wall. Floral motifs were popular, centred on the flaps, with a continuous border carried all the way round the edge. Sometimes another spray of flowers was painted in the middle of the central leaf to balance the design and to mark the spot where a bowl of fruit or vase of flowers or a candlestick could stand.

A table like this would usually be accompanied by a set of chairs in a similar style, also painted, but often in a different but complementary colour. Our pale-grey table shown below might well be accompanied, for instance, by a set of yellow chairs with cabriole legs and checked seat covers, like the one shown on p.112. This arrangement would be more typical of the furniture of the rural gentry. A peasant home would probably have a couple of benches drawn up either side of the table, with a big carver at one end for the man of the house. Generally speaking, however, folding tables were regarded as something of a status symbol. The poorest peasants ate and worked at a sturdy slab of scrubbed pine propped on massive legs or trestles. This would stand next to a window to make the most of any natural light, with a long bench seat built-in along the window wall.

The drop-leaf table was not always set up in the middle of a room space with the chairs all round it. For meals for two or three only it was enough to extend one flap, saving effort as well as space. At once practical, versatile and elegant, the Gustavian drop-leaf dining table shown in our project epitomizes Scandinavian style at its best.

opposite
This is an exceptionally lavish version of the Scandinavian drop-leaf table decorated to useable, elaborate marquetry. The 'tapestry' hanging behind is another elaborate imitation, stippled on canvas rather than woven from wool.

left
This dining room in a small Baroque manor in the province of Jamuland shows a drop-leaf table extended and surrounded with typical sturdy high-backed chairs. Note the corner siting of the fireplace.

Step-by-step

The drop-leaf table we chose for this project is another item from a range of high-quality reproduction Swedish furniture, made from a particularly close grained pine almost free of knots. Our example has the curving cabriole-style legs characteristic of Gustavian Rococo, plus small drawers on either side for cutlery, candles or table linen. The styling here is more elegant than that of conventional gate-leg tables: this table when opened out makes a generous oval shape which will comfortably sit eight people. We decided on a neutral pale-grey finish, using a thinned oil-based paint which allows the wood grain to show through while masking any knots. Oil-based paint, sealed with varnish, seemed the right choice for a piece like a table which will need frequent wiping down as it is more durable than water-based paint. The delicate 'feather' decoration was added freehand, using acrylic tube colour with a little Flow Enhancer added for smooth, easy brushstrokes.

Materials Check-list

- ✦ Standard 50/50 mix of orange and bleached shellac
- ✦ Glider brush
- ✦ 500ml standard white oil-based undercoat
- ✦ Artists' oil colours for tinting grey (raw umber, yellow ochre and black)
- ✦ Standard paint brush
- ✦ White spirit
- ✦ Measuring tape or rule
- ✦ Compass or craft knife
- ✦ White Aquarelleable pencil
- ✦ Acrylic tube paints for 'feather' decoration (alizarin crimson, ultramarine or cobalt blue, burnt umber)
- ✦ Sable brushes – round and lining
- ✦ Antiquing glaze made by adding raw umber acrylic to acrylic scumble
- ✦ Craig and Rose Extra Pale Dead Flat Varnish

1

After it had been sealed with one coat of our standard shellac mixture and smoothed down with fine sandpaper, the table was ready for the first thinned coat of paint. For the pale grey matt finish, I mixed lamp-black, a little raw umber and a little yellow ochre artists' oil colour into ordinary white oil-based undercoat. This was thinned with white spirit to make a paint opaque enough to give an even grey tone, but transparent enough to let the wood grain 'ghost' through. The grey paint was applied with the grain, using a standard 2½in. (6.5cm) brush. When dry, the pale grey looked patchy and a second thin coat was applied to even it up. The underside of the drop leaves were painted at this stage.

2

A continuous inset border design of feathery brushstrokes was sketched in on the dry painted surface with a white Aquarelleable pencil. Use a set of compasses in a fixed position to score a faint guideline all around the table which you can follow. Make sure that the central motif on the drop leaves is dead centre by marking the centre of the central panel, then extending the point with a tape or steel rule out to the extremity of the drop leaves in the extended position.

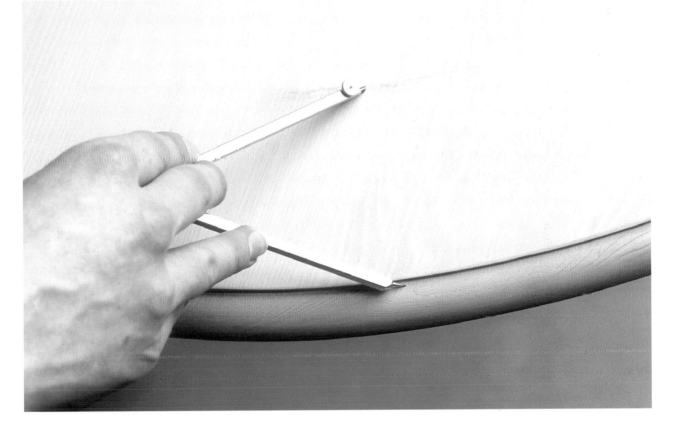

3

Mix a deep mulberry shade of acrylic colour, using ultramarine, alizarin and a little burnt umber. An egg-cupful is sufficient for such a light, feathery design. A little Flow Enhancer makes the paint brush on more fluently, a necessity with a design like this. A round sable and a longer lining sable watercolour brush were used for the motifs. A simple design like this depends for its charm on quick, confident brushwork; it is sensible to practise first on a board. The mulberry paint should look near-transparent in places.

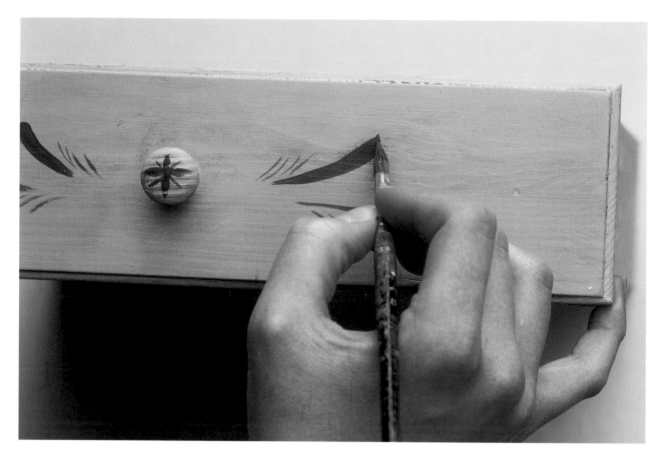

4
Using a deeper version of the mulberry (more blue and burnt umber), the 'feathers' are lightly shaded to make them more emphatic.

5
When quite dry, an antiquing glaze was mixed, using raw umber and a dot of black in acrylic scumble. This was applied in a brush-on, wipe-off technique, to leave just a nuance of darker colour overall.

6
Varnish to seal and protect with Craig and Rose Extra Pale Dead Flat varnish.

Chest of Drawers

with grisaille decoration

Purists may object that the style of grisaille decoration shown on my own very modest pitchpine chest of drawers is not typically Scandinavian. They may be right in that the inspiration for it comes from a page torn out of a copy of *The World of Interiors* several years ago showing rooms largely inspired and decorated by the late John Fowler, the distinguished interior designer. The piece I particularly liked in one of his designs was a pretty Rococo writing desk, exuberantly decorated with grisaille scrolls and floral motifs on a deep blue background. The desk, presumably softwood (or it would not have been painted), might well have been Scandinavian or Austrian.

Fowler himself had been strongly attracted to the Scandinavian mélange of grand and homely, which he christened 'shabby chic', thereby anticipating by several decades a look that has become so fashionable in the nineties. His partner, Nancy Lancaster, introduced him to a whole range of Scandinavian decorating ideas: check linen, painted 'faux' panelling, crystal chandeliers paired stylishly with rush matting or bare boards – a style that combined freshness and prettiness with irreverence and wit. Under Fowler's influence, the 'standard' country house décor, often consisting of chilly 'Adam' green or blue picked out in white and gold, packed with excellent but 'brown' furniture and hung with faded chintz, developed a friendlier character. Soft, warm tones of apricot, yellow or buff began to appear. Neutral floor coverings, sometimes rush matting, replaced wall-to-wall

Wilton or Turkey carpet. The traditional chintz gave way to more sophisticated 'plains', while the family pictures were re-hung and the ornaments rearranged.

Unawed by precedent and history, Fowler had the tact and imagination to coax a highly conservative clientèle into rethinking the stately home in terms of interiors which were more relaxed, less coldly grand, yet at the same time a more stylish setting for their inherited treasures. He was indeed one of the first important decorators to recognize the freshness and charm of the historic Scandinavian style, a good half century before the rest of us.

So whether or not the 'Fowlerish' painted desk is strictly Scandinavian, or maybe a touch Austrian, seems of less importance than the undoubted fact that it draws upon a decorative painting style that influenced furniture painters in all the European countries around the mid eighteenth century. Norwegian 'rosmålning', Austrian 'bauernmalerei', Swedish 'Rococo' are all national developments of a French decorative style that captivated the whole of Europe. Its lightness and grace were to remain powerful influences on peasant art, as the style percolated through the layers of society over the next century or so. The immediately recognizable 'signature' of such work is the asymmetrical scroll, the lively brushstroke which fills a space, frames a motif or encircles a box lid. In decorative terms it is a brave departure from the tightly organized, often geometrical design which preceded the style. Of all the Scandinavian regions where Rococo penetrated, the south of Sweden, Skane, seems to have captured its spirit best at the peasant level. There, sky-blue painted cupboards and chests were, typically, decorated with rose garlands enclosed by a froth of grisaille scrollwork, expressing a light-hearted *joie de vivre* – a delightful episode in Scandinavian peasant art.

opposite
Not specifically 'grisaille', but very much a folk interpretation of European 'Rococo' in its swirling arabesques, this photograph shows a wonderfully vivid paint treatment applied to the gable walls of an old Norwegian log cabin.

Step-by-step

I have had the small pine chest of drawers shown here for years, always intending to decorate it some day. I felt that the Rococo design would look pretty, though it would need some adapting from a desk to a chest of drawers. The colour scheme of shades of red, with grisaille, was chosen to fit in with my bedroom's colours – a strong green on the walls and curtains – rather than because it is authentic for the style and period. On the whole, Rococo pieces were painted in pale, rather feminine pastel shades; straw-yellow, shell-pink, cerulean-blue and almond-green as a background to scrolling brushwork and 'rocaille' motifs. However, I must say that my bolder colour scheme works very well and has completely transformed the pine chest.

Materials Check-list

- ✦ 500ml Barn Red Woodwash
- ✦ Nutshell red oxide powder pigment
- ✦ Caput Mortuum powder pigment
- ✦ Hogshair fitch for colour mixing
- ✦ White Aquarelleable pencil by Schwan
- ✦ Liquitex Flow Enhancer
- ✦ Sable brushes, sizes 1 and 4
- ✦ Standard 2 in. (5cm) paint brush
- ✦ Fine sandpaper
- ✦ 500ml Mulberry Woodwash
- ✦ Tracing paper
- ✦ Craig and Rose Extra Pale Dead Flat Varnish

1

The old chest of drawers had been stripped of treacly black stain years ago and now only needed a rub down with wire wool and white spirit to remove wax, grease or dirt. The brass handles were removed at the same time. A 'true red' water-based acrylic paint was mixed, using Barn Red Woodwash with two powder pigments, red oxide (which the Swedes call 'English red') and Caput Mortuum, a dusky purple-brown, dissolved in a little water and well mixed, then tested on a board. Two coats were needed for a solid cover (red is not the colour for semi-transparent finishes) and both coats were lightly rubbed down when dry for smoothness, as water paint slightly 'raises' the wood grain.

2

The grisaille motifs are sketched in using white Aquarelleable pencil by Schwan. This can be rubbed off with a damp rag if necessary. The design features grisaille floral motifs with darker red panels edged with Rococo S-curves and bold lining. The panels are outlined first with S-curves and 'telephone' shapes, using a Size 4 watercolour brush and standard white emulsion with Liquitex Flow Enhancer added to give 'slip' and freedom to the brushstrokes. Practice these shapes first on a board. The brush is 'plopped' down almost vertically for the dot, then swirled to make a neat circle and trailed smoothly into the S-bend, ending with the same procedure in reverse.

3

When the white decoration is dry, fill in the outlined panels (which is where the brass handles are positioned) with a darker, plummy red as shown. I used Mulberry Woodwash for this, a fat fitch for the main infilling, and the size 4 brush for taking the colour neatly up to the S-bends.

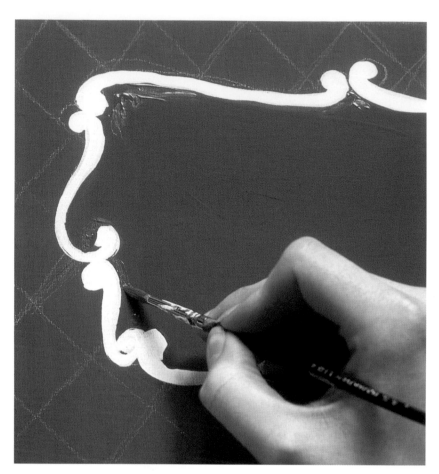

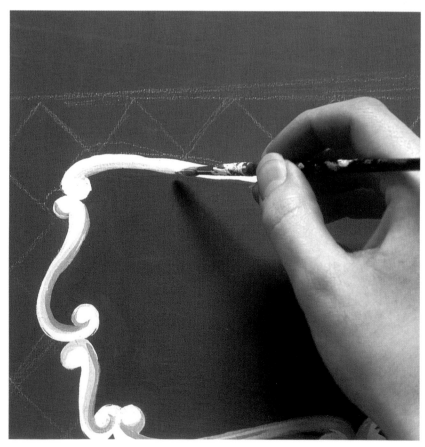

4

Mix a little lamp-black gouache into one corner of the previous emulsion flow enhancer mixture to create a range of greys (pale, medium and nearly black). Use these to 'shadow' the S-curves, as shown.

5

The same brush and paint mixtures are used for lining, as shown. Start with a broad white line, following the pencilled guidelines, and shade with mid grey, then more emphatically with dark grey. Flow Enhancer makes this lining, which can be quite crude, slip along smoothly. Keep your eyes fixed just ahead of the brush for a confident, controlled stroke. A few strokes of near black will dramatize your curves and outlining.

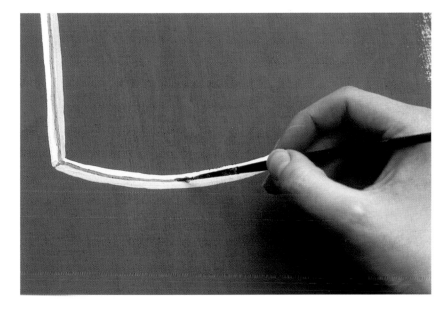

6

Check that all the floral motifs line up vertically down the drawer fronts. Motifs can be copied freehand or photocopied (enlarging to suit the space) and traced off, using tracing paper rubbed over with Aquarelleable pencil on the back. This leaves a distinct enough guideline which can be further defined by hand.

7

Paint in all the floral motifs (leaves, sprays, etc.) with mid grey first, using the size 4 brush for the larger rounded petals and a no.1 sable from the Pro Arte range (longer bristles for slender leaves and flicks) for the stems, grasses and finer detail. Use pure white to highlight certain leaves, stems, petals and to outline some flower shapes. Use dark grey or black to give light emphasis to certain motifs here and there. Stand back to judge where the designs need more highlighting or more dark contrast. The effect aimed at should be delicate, almost 'ghostly', like old lace on a dark background.

8

Carry on with the grisaille 'lining' round all main surfaces, as shown in the finished piece (see principal illustration opposite). Add (this is optional but makes for a pretty effect) a light lattice-work of pale grey lines on the plum-red panels, adding a little cross where the lattice intersects. Use a 1 in. (2.5cm) brush, dipped in the white mixture then brushed out until almost dry, to add 'dry-brushed' touches of white around the floral motifs.

9

Varnish all over with two coats of Craig and Rose Extra Pale Dead Flat Varnish, rubbing down lightly when dry for a smooth but matt, non-yellowing protective finish. Replace the handles.

Gustavian Writing Table

with naïve 'trompe-l'œil' decoration

Trompe-l'œil has always been one of the most immediately seductive of all decorative painting techniques. There is an element of theatrical trickery and humour about painted images which appear to be three-dimensional at first glance, only to dissolve into the painted surface and reveal their imposture as you move to left or right. The technique, indeed, has a long history. Taken in its widest sense, to mean any painted imitation of another more expensive material – marble, lapis lazuli, carved stone – *trompe-l'œil* has been widely used since Classical times. The Romans made much use of 'faux marbre' in their villas, and painted 'still lifes' with deliberate realism on the walls of their dwellings, choosing food pictures for the dining room, erotic subjects for the bedroom and so on. But the Roman use of *trompe-l'œil* was primitive compared to the super-realism employed by late Renaissance artists like Veronese in his decoration of the interiors of Palladio's villas. By the time of the Renaissance, painting techniques had much advanced and understanding of perspective, foreshortening and chiaroscuro proved invaluable in *trompe-l'œil* work wherever great realism was intended. Painters would undertake to reproduce painted architecture, loggias, columns or statuary – the whole repertoire of luxurious princely palaces – on the flat walls of the not-so-grand country villa of a family with aspirations.

In time, this fashion for painted trickery spread throughout Europe, reaching Scandinavia, as usual, a little belatedly. The Swedes, in particular, turned

trompe-l'œil to their own purposes. 'Imitation-målning' ('faux' finishes and *trompe-l'œil*) became fashionable in palaces, public buildings (old churches are full of astonishing visual flights of fancy) and the homes of the nobility. The Baroque period saw painted walls imitating tapestries, painted ceilings imitating moulded stucco and painted dados, pillars, and pews imitating marble. Queen Margrethe of Denmark, herself an artist in various media, has explained this liking for 'imitation-målning' quite simply. The Scandinavian countries, she says, were always relatively poor and relatively remote, so were driven to imitate in paint the noble materials and princely effects of southern Europe.

One of the most sophisticated examples of *trompe-l'œil* in Scandinavia is an anteroom painted for the Royal Tutor and Court Architect to Gustav II by the Court painter, Johan Pasch. The walls display the owner's interests, activities and favourite possessions, including a pet monkey and a pug dog, the whole painted with brilliant realism and charm to form a sort of portrait 'in absentia'. The *trompe-l'œil* is elegant and accomplished, yet the simply coloured walls and whitewashed chimneypiece designate it a modest room. It is this juxtaposition of the grand with the humble, or at least unpretentious, which is so characteristic of Scandinavian style and one of the reasons, I believe, for its increasing popularity today.

This example is the work of a skilled and experienced professional artist and outside the scope of all but the most talented amateurs. But *trompe-l'œil* can also be charming, even if somewhat less effective, when executed in a naïve or even primitive manner. Examples of such work abound throughout Scandinavia and we have taken an especially appealing one as the inspiration for our *trompe-l'œil* writing table.

opposite

Simple and elegant, this Gustavian writing desk has an allure which has much to do with its aristocratic 18th century provenance. With stacked pigeonholes to one side, they were designed to stand between long windows, to make the most of natural light.

Step-by-step

Swedish reproduction pieces, such as this, are made of excellent quality pine, with few knots and tight grain. But they should be 'prepped' for further decoration with two coats of shellac, lightly sanded when dry. Lower-grade surfaces, with knots, splits, cracks, etc., should be filled and rubbed smooth with sandpaper. Old varnish should be stripped to give a 'key' for paint, or at least sanded back thoroughly. This is an ambitious project and needs careful preparation to give the best results.

Materials Check-list

- ✦ Dark grey standard undercoat
- ✦ 500ml Mulberry flat oil paint
- ✦ 500ml each of button polish and white polish
- ✦ Methylated spirit
- ✦ White spirit (for brush cleaning)
- ✦ Fine grade sandpaper and extra-fine wire wool
- ✦ White Aquarelleable pencil by Schwan
- ✦ Gold acrylic paint
- ✦ Encre de Chine Intense by Le Franc Bourgeois
- ✦ White acrylic primer or white acrylic gesso
- ✦ Standard white oil-based undercoat
- ✦ Brushes: standard 2 in. (5cm) paintbrush, 2 in. (5cm) glider, 4 in. (10cm) glider or fitch, one extra fine sable, one fine sable with longer hairs for lining
- ✦ Raw umber artist acrylic (optional)
- ✦ 1 spool red car body tape
- ✦ 500ml Craig and Rose Eggshell Varnish
- ✦ Rottenstone
- ✦ Rags, saucers, glass jars

1

The first coat of mulberry-tinted flat oil paint is brushed on over a dark grey standard undercoat. After 24 hours this coat is lightly sanded all over with fine grade abrasive paper, brushed down and re-coated, the paint being applied as smoothly as possible using a 2 in. (5cm) glider brush (see p.16). Allow to dry for 24 hours.

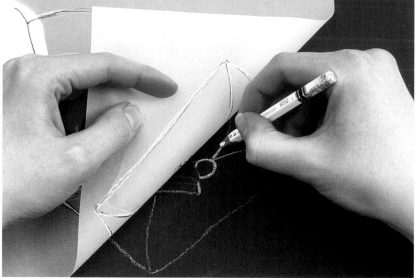

2

After more light sanding and dusting down, position the trompe-l'œil motifs. These can be enlarged on a photocopier and then traced off (rub the back of the paper with the white Aquarelleable pencil, then draw round outlines firmly) or copied freehand on to the table top with the same white pencil. Rule a line set in approximately 3 in. (7.5cm) from the table edge. This will be gilded. The motifs can be re-arranged to suit your space. It may help to cut the shapes in paper and try different arrangements.

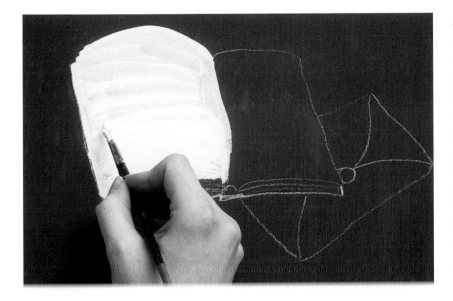

3

Next fill in all the shapes carefully with white acrylic primer, acrylic gesso, or standard white oil-based undercoat. Use a 1 in. (2.5cm) brush to fill the space roughly, then tidy the outlines with a fine sable brush. Allow it to dry hard, then sand back lightly with fine grade paper and re-coat. A third coat – use undercoat this time – may be needed to give a flat, even, white finish, but try to avoid too much build-up of paint on the motifs.

4

Use gold paint and a fine brush to add touches of gold on the book pages as shown, on the tea cup and saucer and around the spectacle frames. Allow it to dry.

5

Now, using the finest sable brushes and Encre de Chine Intense by Le Franc Bourgeois, start drawing in the black outlines, 'writing' and other details, aiming for the look of an old woodcut. Shading is done by cross-hatching, as in a pen and ink drawing, or with fine parallel lines. A certain crudeness about the drawing is quite appropriate; these renderings are, after all, supposed to be 'naïve', and the unrealistic perspective adds to their charm.

6

The Encre de Chine must be left for 24 hours to harden, otherwise the first coat of shellac will create horrible smudges. Go over the entire table top, legs, etc. with a 50-50 mixture of white polish (bleached shellac) and button polish, diluted with a splash of methylated spirit. Use a 2in. (5cm) glider to 'float' the shellac (a thin spirit varnish) fast and smoothly over the trompe-l'oeil motifs, avoiding too much re-brushing, since this gives a strong yellowish build-up. Leave several hours to harden, then rub back gently with extra fine wire wool (000 grade) to even out streakiness and smooth the surfaces. Brush any dust away.

7

The gilt edge line can be tackled in several ways. A fine, ¹/₂in.(1.5cm) sable brush with slightly longer hairs can be used to run it on freehand, using the table edge as a support. The shellac

sealing coat means mistakes can be wiped off quickly. Alternatively, use a smooth length of wood approximately 2in. (5cm) thick as an improvised ruler. Finally cheat, by placing red car tape as shown and painting over the gap. Masking tape does not have enough adhesion and some paint will always creep underneath, giving a muzzy line. The same techniques can be used to outline drawers, as shown.

8

For a rich, mellow eighteenth-century finish, give the whole piece at least four or five more coats of the white polish/button polish mixture as before. If the motifs are yellowing too much, apply these in white polish only. Rub down with fine wire wool between every second coat, dusting scrupulously to remove the fine particles. As a final protection against water, alcohol, etc., give the piece a final coat of Craig and Rose Eggshell Varnish which is tougher than shellac. Rub this down with a paste of rottenstone in water, applied with a soft rag using a circular polishing motion. Clean off. Buff up with a soft cloth.

Tray

with 'combed' decoration using buttermilk glaze or paint

One unexpected recent trend in decoration is a small but strong revival of interest in traditional or primitive paints, such as distemper, limewash and casein-based paints, all of which were in common use in Scandinavia until the nineteen-fifties, when easy-to-use emulsions swept the board. However, all that long experience of making up low-cost but pleasing paints from whatever ingredients were to hand lives on in the work of Scandinavian decorative painters. They make frequent use of all these old paints in their work, but also have the advantage of a knowledge of recent paint technology. The current popularity of these time-honoured paints has a lot to do with environmental concerns and anxiety about the toxicity of some ingredients of oil-based commercial paint. Aesthetic considerations come into the picture, too. Compared with the lifeless, pasty colour and texture of most standard commercial paints, due to their 'plastic' content and additives designed to give one-coat results, the home-made alternatives offer the appeal of purer colour, interesting texture and a 'country' look which people find refreshing and attractive.

Buttermilk (casein) makes an interesting glaze, as we found while working on this project. Not having access to a dairy herd or to a butter-maker's, we had to buy our buttermilk from a health food shop. In rural Scandinavia, the main ingredient would have been either to hand on the farm or somewhere close by in the locality. Buttermilk is the thin, but casein-rich liquid left over after churning cream for butter. It mixes readily with powdered pigments to create a firm but malleable glaze with a lot of 'body', ideal for the vigorous, rustic graining shown here. For graining purposes just enough pigment is added to create a definite but slightly translucent colour; for an opaque paint, which was also used on walls and furniture, one would add some chalk, for opacity, and more pigment. To create a truly durable exterior paint, tough enough to withstand Nordic winters, lime putty was added as well as a host of 'secret' ingredients, which varied from village to village and painter to painter. These might have included urine, vitriol and seaweed. The 'falun rott', or rich and vivid red-brown exterior paint seen on wooden buildings throughout Sweden, is claimed to last for anything from twelve to thirty years.

Our buttermilk glaze is in a different league, but its simplicity and 'green' appeal should make it attractive enough. Like the Austrian 'kleister' preparation, which uses cornflour rather than buttermilk, it produces a glaze which brushes out smoothly and responds splendidly to the sort of combing and stamping effects which are the mark of nineteenth-century rustic graining. We used 'combs' snipped out of plastic containers, a re-cycling tip which you might find – ironically – appropriate. The glaze dries quite quickly, but if you are dissatisfied with your handiwork, it can be washed off again with a scouring pad and water. Obviously, it must be sealed with a waterproof, oil-based varnish. We used Craig and Rose Extra Pale Dead Flat Varnish, which is an alkyd varnish. Acrylic varnish dissolves the glaze and should be avoided. In time, I suspect, a buttermilk glaze – or paint – will harden sufficiently to stand wiping down, but a tray will always need extra protection.

opposite
Buttermilk glaze is unusually 'solid', lending itself to the swoops and swirls created by home-made combs, all of which are well displayed on this neat and useful piece from a nineteenth-century peasant interior.

Step-by-step

You can hardly get more 'country' than buttermilk paint, and this project is a lively reminder that, for hard-pressed folk in remote rural areas, necessity was truly the mother of invention. Buttermilk, the non-fatty residue of butter churning, is a crude form of casein, a durable binder and medium for dry pigment, to which painters sometimes added lime for hardness. Commercial buttermilk, as sold today in health-food stores, makes an interesting paint or glaze, with a slippery but firm consistency which is a natural medium for combed decoration.

People sometimes worry that it will 'go off' and smell cheesy. All I can say is that, in normal warm conditions, it dries quite fast and without any hint of 'off' smells. Of course, buttermilk paint or glaze needs fixing when dry with an appropriate varnish, though if left untouched for long enough it develops quite a tough surface of its own. But for a tray, which is our project here, extra protection is absolutely necessary.

Materials Check-list

- ✦ 1 carton buttermilk
- ✦ Red oxide and ochre powder pigment
- ✦ White matt emulsion, tinted cream with ochre pigment
- ✦ Matt acrylic varnish
- ✦ Plastic card
- ✦ Scalpel or scissors
- ✦ Standard brush
- ✦ Craig and Rose Eggshell Varnish

1

The tray is first painted over in a warm cream matt emulsion. Two coats were applied and these were then lightly rubbed back to smooth. The painted tray is then given one quick-drying coat of matt acrylic varnish to give a smooth, tight finish for the glaze.

2
A red-gold glaze is mixed with red oxide and ochre powder pigments (dissolved first in a little water) then mixed well with buttermilk until smooth and evenly coloured.

3
The buttermilk glaze is brushed evenly over the base of the tray. A 'comb', cut from plastic card with scissors as shown, is dashed in a scalloping, scooping movement across the glaze, revealing the cream base and creating attractive shapes.

4

The canted sides of the tray were glazed and decorated last, after the base had dried, to prevent smudging.

5

You can have fun with this technique, trying any shape that takes your fancy: lattice-work, gingham-type checks, squiggles, circles. If the glaze seems to be hardening up, either brush on a new layer or, if too dry, sponge with warm water, clean and start again.

6

When hard dry (overnight) the whole tray was given a coat of Craig and Rose Eggshell Varnish (avoid acrylic varnish which dissolves the buttermilk glaze). Brass handles were then screwed to both sides.

Baltic Secretaire

with glazed, dragged finish

I found and bought the piece illustrated in an antique shop in Bath, Somerset. I particularly admired the handsome lines of this overgrown desk and, because it was already painted, I realized that it could be 'tweaked' to fit into my own East London study/ workroom which was decorated in the moody blues and reds of what I then fondly believed to be 'Williamsburg' colours.

I had no idea, then, that this obviously un-English piece belonged to a distinct stylistic family of furniture making, showing influences from Germany and Russia which themselves harked back to the Neoclassicism of late eighteenth-century Italy. Then, in a saleroom catalogue, I spotted the second cousin of my desk/bureau and realized that it belonged to the distinct category designated as 'Baltic'. The Baltic states (Estonia, Latvia and Lithuania) lie along the Baltic Sea across the waters from Scandinavia. The nearest relations to my 'secretaire' I had ever seen had been in Denmark, where such monumental but still friendly forms can be frequentrly found in early nineteenth-century pieces, invariably in mahogany or mahogany veneer. Their main family characteristic is a certain 'stripped' Neoclassicism in the curved or 'bombé' cupboard fronts and in such obvious Neoclassical detailing as the pediment and curved pilasters. At the same time the clever construction of such features as a sliding, rather than roll-front, curved desk lid implied a local familiarity and skill in solving joinery problems. All these are commonplace in the best Baltic furniture.

My piece is some way down the social scale, being veneered rather than solid mahogany. The carcase is pine which, as often happens with softwood, was riddled with woodworm. The irony of this piece appearing in a book about painted furniture is that it was clearly not intended to be painted in the first place. Made in the early nineteenth century, in the full flush of European enthusiasm for mahogany, it was obviously surfaced originally with a mahogany veneer. Then the softwood carcase was invaded by woodworm and the veneer began to flake off. Rather than repair the original finish, some ingenious person felt it would be simpler, as is often the case, to fill any holes and cracks and to paint the piece. The result is a curiously attractive article of furniture, to which I merely added a dark glaze and some gilt lining to bring it into my existing colour scheme. Since being alerted to this type of furniture, as often happens, I have come across many more examples. The most recent was a version in stripped pine which has pride of place in a rustic but glamorous kitchen in Spain designed by Jaime Parladé, one of the most internationally celebrated of current Spanish interior designers. There, against ochre-yellow walls partly tiled in the blue-and-white Moorish-style, it stands filled with splendid Spanish ceramics, looking entirely at home and in command of the situation.

opposite
A small writing desk and antique chair get their unmistakably 'old Swedish' look from their moody blue paintwork, whose patina stems from many thin coats of hand-mixed paint subjected to at least a century of use.

left
Another charming small desk, in the Rococo idiom, with rounded top and cabriole legs, acquires its particular style and character from an old paint finish worn away over the years.

Step-by-step

A very dark, almost black, oil glaze is a great enhancer of the thundery blues and rusty reds that keep cropping up on Scandinavian painted pieces. It should be well thinned with white spirit and brushed out very finely with a 1¹/₂-2 in. (3.5-5cm) brush so that the brushmarks are barely visible and follow the grain of the wood beneath. The dark but transparent glaze completely transforms the existing colours – here a light denim-blue and brown-red – adding depth and complexity as well as blending contrasting colours together.

In the case of the secretaire shown here, it also dramatically emphasizes the unusual bombé or curved doors and sliding top, providing built-in shading. You can suit yourself as to whether you use traditional oil-based media throughout or, as we did, for speed, a mixture of fast-drying acrylics for the base colours, with oil glaze and oil-based varnish to finish up with. Oil glaze has the edge over acrylic scumble glaze on a piece this size, where the object is to achieve a very fine, even, dragged finish over quite large surfaces. The oil glaze 'sets up' more slowly and can be brushed out more thinly.

Materials Check-list

- ✦ Acrylic primer (optional)
- ✦ Mid-blue acrylic paint (made with matt white emulsion tinted with Windsor blue, a very little raw umber and black acrylic or gouache)
- ✦ Light-brown red acrylic, made with burnt sienna acrylic plus a pinch of red oxide powder colour (don't add any white to this mix as it makes 'knicker pink'; add raw sienna to lighten if necessary)
- ✦ Masking tape
- ✦ Pencil
- ✦ Straight edge or steel rule
- ✦ Sandpaper
- ✦ Fine wire wool
- ✦ Shellac mixture (50/50 button polish and white polish)
- ✦ Methylated spirit
- ✦ Transparent oil (or scumble) glaze
- ✦ Raw umber, burnt umber, lamp black artists' oil tube colour
- ✦ Standard paint brushes (one 1¹/₂ in. [4cm] and one 2 in. [5cm])
- ✦ Glider for dragging
- ✦ Gold acrylic paint (optional)
- ✦ Lining brush
- ✦ Craig and Rose Eggshell Varnish

1

A mid-blue acrylic paint is shown here brushed directly on to bare wood. If the wood surface is coarse in texture or requires filling, it is best to apply a coat of acrylic primer first, lightly sanded when dry. Two coats of blue will be needed to give an opaque colour. Both need rubbing down when dry.

2

Rust-red paint has been used to pick out mouldings and run a contrasting edge round drawers and desk top. Use masking tape to mask off areas to be painted red, as shown, then apply brown-red acrylic paint made from burnt sienna with a little red oxide powder pigment added for depth.

3

One coat of shellac (50 per cent button polish, 50 per cent white polish, plus a splash of methylated spirit) was applied overall, after removing the masking tape and doing any tidying-up brushwork needed. The shellac coat sealed the acrylic colours, providing a smoother, non-absorbent base over which the oil glaze could be dragged. It also softened the original colours, giving the chalky blue a greenish cast.

4

When the shellac was fully dry (allow 4-6 hours, or overnight where possible) the oil glaze was made up, using approximately eight parts raw umber to one part burnt umber to one part black artists' oil tube colour, dissolved in white spirit with a stiff fitch brush, then mixed with enough transparent oil glaze to give a thin, runny, cream-like consistency.

Test the colour first on a board or an inconspicuous surface, keeping a rag dampened with white spirit ready to eliminate any mistakes. When the colour is right, test it for consistency. Brush the glaze on thinly, leave a couple of minutes, then re-brush, using a clean brush and holding the brush as shown, index finger keeping it steady to produce fine clean stripes. If the stripes blur almost immediately, the glaze is too thin; add more oil glaze, mixing well. If the stripes look too hard and dark, there may be too much tint; add more oil glaze and solvent. If the stripes look 'ridgy', then you have too much oil glaze; add more solvent.

When the glaze is satisfactory, begin dragging over the whole piece, taking one facet at a time. Brush on glaze thinly and evenly, then re-brush with a clean dry brush (wipe on an old towel) in steady parallel strokes from top to bottom, going over red and blue in the same operation. Rather than glaze over a large area, with the risk of the glaze 'setting up' before you can drag the whole surface, it may be better to glaze and drag a section at a time, but much depends on how quickly you work.

5

The secretaire still looked a touch austere and I therefore felt a discreet touch of dull gilt lining would lift it. I used a lining brush and gold metallic paint (acrylic) for this, running the lines on freehand, with a wooden straight-edge for support. When the gold lines were hard dry, I dirtied them with more of the dark glaze, brushing it over the gold lines with a fine brush.

6

Oil glaze gradually dries quite hard, hard enough to wipe down with a damp cloth for instance. But a piece of furniture such as a desk is subject to a lot of heavy wear so, as a precaution, I gave the bureau two coats of Craig and Rose Eggshell Varnish, both applied smoothly and rubbed down carefully when dry, using fine-grade sandpaper.

Double-fronted Cupboard
with Rococo rustic decoration

Almost every Scandinavian country cottage, farm or modest house would own at least one capacious 'skåp', or cupboard, of the type shown here. Sometimes they have two doors, sometimes four, sometimes a cupboard below is topped by shelves for displaying china or pots and pans, rather like our own kitchen dressers. In some cases, such a cupboard was an add-on component of a free-standing bed. The bed itself would be demurely curtained and tucked into a corner, while the cupboard formed an overgrown 'tailboard'. This faced the rest of the room and, with the bed curtains drawn, the 'skåp' would thus appear to be a real item of furniture and help to dispel any impression of 'bedroomy' intimacy.

This sort of ingenious, multi-purpose furniture is a truly Scandinavian peasant invention, born, doubtless, from the exigencies of family life in one room – in many cottages families ate, worked and slept in the one heated room – and a proud wish to maintain a seemly appearance despite such a cramped existence. In some of the more extreme versions of the bed-with-additions, not only does the bed conclude with a substantial 'skåp' but a tall-case clock might be built into the corner at right-angles to the cupboard.

The shared characteristics of such country pieces are softwood construction and a painted finish. This can be quite plain – deep-blue or brown-red being popular colours – but more often they are ebulliently decorated. Where the painted decoration has a stiff, tentative air about it, with a quaint little nosegay

opposite
Solid, capacious pieces like this lovingly constructed and lavishly decorated bureau-cum-armoire from a Swedish farmhouse show how much thought and pride went into the furnishing of quite modest homes.

plumped in the exact centre of a door panel perhaps, it is possible that this was work done by an amateur, perhaps the householders themselves or someone in the neighbourhood with experience of making up paints and grinding colours, such as a boatbuilder or carpenter. The repertoire of motifs is often limited, although it may include the stylized marbling or Rococo swirls which more practised painters worked up on their sample boards to attract custom.

Certain regional styles of decoration – 'rosmålning' from Norway, or the distinctive 'kurbits' motifs from the Swedish province of Dalarna – are immediately recognizable. They have a bold fluency of execution which marks them as 'professional' work, bearing in mind that 'professional' in this context did not necessarily mean that the individuals concerned were decorative painters first and foremost. Sometimes this was a job combined with a second, seasonal trade, such as fishing, logging or husbandry and, in Sweden especially, soldiering.

Soldier-painters, indeed, are a Swedish oddity, a legacy of a feudal system where trained soldiers were kept as a permanent reserve to be available when the need arose, but who were free to boost their income by odd-jobbing in the meantime. That so many took to decorative painting is another oddity, usually explained by the fact that campaigning soldiers travelling abroad were exposed to sophisticated influences unimaginable to toiling peasants whose entire lives might be passed hundreds of miles from a big city and whose energies were absorbed by the hard graft of their daily existence. But whatever the context of the decorative work, one fact is undeniable: these Nordic people adored colour first and dashing, decorative sleight-of-hand next. It was a serious and important adventure for them to commission such work in their homes.

Step-by-step

Suzanne Martin, who has worked on many projects for this book, is Swedish herself and has had considerable experience in painting antique and reproduction Scandinavian pieces for shops and private clients. The 'skänk-skåp' shown is a family possession which she has been intending to decorate in colours chosen to suit her kitchen, which has a green and red theme, rather than in any specific traditional style or colour scheme. An allergy to solvents, brought on by working with oil-based paints, has led her to experiment with water-based equivalents, which happen to be the current state-of-the-art products. She currently favours a range of acrylic paints (Galeria) sold in generous containers which she uses both diluted with water or straight from the pot, mixing to create more shades and occasionally 'tweaking' a colour with artists' quality gouache or acrylic tube colours.

This 'skåp' is a handsome well-proportioned piece with a heavy Baroque cornice and door-panels with mouldings. The cupboard, which had probably been painted at some point, was stripped. It was given one coat of shellac all over, lightly rubbed back when dry. This was to seal any knots, help fill the grain and present a good surface for paint.

Materials Check-list

- ✦ Shellac
- ✦ Sandpaper
- ✦ Galeria acrylic paints (cobalt blue, cadmium red, yellow ochre, raw umber, titanium white)
- ✦ Steel graining comb
- ✦ 3 in. (7.5cm) brush
- ✦ Fine sable brush for decorative details
- ✦ English red powder pigment
- ✦ PVA
- ✦ Craig and Rose Eggshell and Extra Pale Dead Flat Varnishes

1

Suzanne mixed a soft sage-green using ochre, cobalt and a spot of red, 'tweaked' with a little white and raw umber for mellowness. This was her base paint, which she diluted with enough water to make a paint just opaque enough to cover knots without masking the grain completely. She used a 3 in. (7.5cm) brush. The green was used to cover everything apart from the panel mouldings, cornice and central plinth.

2

With a darker green made by adding more cobalt and raw umber, she painted the cornice, base, plinth and panel mouldings, wiping back the mouldings to soften the contrast.

3

The same darker green was brushed quite thickly over the panels, one at a time. While the paint was still wet and soft she used a steel graining comb to mark 'wiggly' lines down the panels, one by one, allowing the paler green base to show through.

4

Using a Scandinavian powder pigment, confusingly called 'English red', mixed with a little diluted PVA as binder, she used her thumb to make streaky 'splodges' at regular intervals round the scooped-out section of the cornice and the flat areas as shown. To create these characteristic Swedish 'thumbmarks' load some colour on to the ball of your thumb, then wipe it off in two or three strokes to create little 'wing' shapes. This is a stylistic device intended to suggest marble.

5

The sides of the 'skåp' are decorated freehand, using a fine brush and the same English red/PVA mixture. The motif, like a fine fringe of festoons linking red circles, is another traditional Swedish motif, with a distinctly Rococo flavour.

6

The flat space below the cornice called out for special emphasis. Using the same red paint and fine brush, Suzanne added some attractive Rococo scroll shapes on either side of a central three-petal flower.

7

Glazing was used to blend colours together, to age them subtly and to emphasize the texture of the painted wood overall. The glaze was made up with a 'dirtier' shade of green to which raw umber was added. This was mixed with diluted PVA, then brushed over the entire cupboard. The glaze was then wiped back here and there with a cloth to even it out and bring up the colour beneath. When fully dry, the whole piece was given two coats of varnish: eggshell first for toughness, followed by Craig and Rose Extra Pale Dead Flat to remove any shine. A light final sanding once the varnish was hard-dry left a sleek surface without hairs, grit or dust, ready for another two hundred years of use.

Blanket Box

decorated in the Almoge folk style

Wooden chests are probably the oldest form of free-standing furniture and certainly the oldest form of storage. Even after more sophisticated types of furniture, such as chests of drawers and wardrobes, became the norm among the upper classes, the Scandinavian peasant household kept clothing, linen or even a young girl's hand-woven, hand-stitched trousseau in massive wooden chests. In many houses these were kept in a 'chest room'. The tradition in Scandinavia of using such chests – 'kista' – dates back at least as far as the twelfth century, when they were decorated with carvings descended from the designs used by the Vikings on their long-boats of dragons and interlacing strap-work. These earliest chests had no lids and some of the early carved decoration does bear faint traces of colour. Painted chests as an important expression of peasant art, however, seem to have appeared much later, during the eighteenth century. Chests from this period tend to be laden with floral motifs and Rococo scrolls on a dark-coloured ground in deep red, blue or green. The owner's initials and the date were invariably worked into the design. Members of the family had their own individual chests for their 'Sunday best' or church-going clothes. Other chests held the embroidered hangings and cushions which were only brought out for special occasions, such as Christmas, funerals or weddings. There were regional differences in chest construction;

central Sweden favoured flat-topped chests, while in the north and south domed lids were popular.

It seems likely that many chests were made and decorated at home. A chest is not a particularly challenging piece to make. The raw material was everywhere to hand and Swedish countrymen were resourceful and practised in simple carpentry. It would be nice to think that their skills extended to the painted decoration: a whole family working on a daughter's bridal chest, for instance. But, on the whole, it seems probable that the family chests were painted by the travelling painters who stayed with the families while they worked on commission, decorating smaller items of furniture as well as walls, cupboard beds and other pieces. For such refurbishment they were often paid in kind – with sacks of grain or flour, or a goose or pig. Unlike the itinerant furniture pedlars, their sleighs piled high with chairs (see p.36), painters could travel light, their pigments, brushes and special tools like combs and stencils stowed in a back-pack. They could usually rely on finding other materials for making up their paints – chalk, lime, linseed oil or buttermilk – on the spot.

Nowadays, the antique chests are valued for their massive dignity and family associations, and for their rich colouring. Many have found their way into museums and many more into the big-city antique shops. Anyone who succumbs to the powerful attraction exerted by these remarkable works of the rural tradition can spend many happy hours visiting the 'kistehuset', or chest room, of Scandinavia's many fascinating folk museums. The book has yet to be written which documents in colour the range of styles, decoration and construction of this simplest of all furnishings, a large wooden box, which the peasant artists' imagination transformed over the centuries into a real 'object of virtue'.

opposite

Painted wooden chests were the earliest form of storage in every Scandinavian home, from palace to cottage. A special 'chest room' was often built on to peasant cottages, doubling as a spare room for guests. As well as holding clothes and bedding, there were chests for storing ceremonial hangings and embroideries brought out only on special occasions.

Step-by-step

An old (but not necessarily Scandinavian) pine blanket box is an ideal subject for richly colourful and flowery decoration in the traditional Scandinavian manner, complete with *trompe-l'œil* hasps and 'Gothic' lettering and date.

    The box was first stripped of any wax or oil by rubbing down with white spirit and wire wool. When it feels smooth and not sticky, and looks visibly lighter, you can take it that it is clean enough.

Materials Check-list

- ◆ Shellac (button polish)
- ◆ Glider brush
- ◆ Methylated spirit
- ◆ Fine sandpaper wrapped round wooden block or scouring pad
- ◆ Woodwash colours (Midnight, Gitane, Maize in sample-pot size with a squeeze of raw umber tube acrylic for base paint)
- ◆ Burnt umber, white emulsion, black acrylic for hasps
- ◆ Barn Red and Olive Woodwash for florals
- ◆ Off-white emulsion and black acrylic for lettering
- ◆ Aquarelleable white pencil
- ◆ Liquitex Flow Enhancer
- ◆ Standard brushes for applying base coat and varnish
- ◆ Fine sable watercolour brushes
- ◆ PVA

1

The first step, as always, is to apply the shellac (plain button polish here) to seal and prepare the wood for paint. A medium, greeny-blue acrylic paint was mixed from three Woodwash colours (Midnight, Gitane and Maize) with a dash of raw umber. This was brushed on to cover most of the piece.

2

Rub back here and there to the wood with fine sandpaper on a block to create an aged effect and variety of texture.

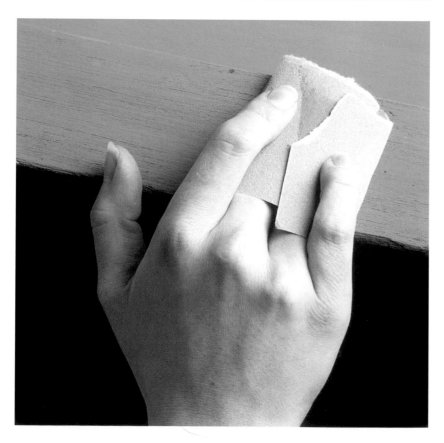

3

Trompe-l'oeil *hasps or corner brackets were added with burnt umber acrylic, using off-white and black to add shadows below and highlights above.*

4

Tulip shapes were sketched in the four corners of the lid and a loose semi-circle of red flowers and leaves on the chest front, using the Aquarelleable white pencil. These were coloured in with a red acrylic for flower shapes, a bright olive for leaves and stems. In the central space the date 'ANNO 1994' and Suzanne's initials 'SM' were sketched in with white pencil.

5

Using black gouache, plus a little PVA for 'stick', plus Liquitex Flow Enhancer, the date and initials were brushed in with fine sable watercolour brushes.

6

Off-white acrylic was used to add flicks of white to flowers, leaves and lettering, a traditional 'folk' touch that adds a vivacious spontaneity to stylized decoration. Keep these light and slender.

7

A coat of button polish diluted with methylated spirit and mixed with raw umber was added to seal and tone down the colours still further. Finally, the 'kistan', now thoroughly Swedish looking, was rubbed down when dry.

Dining Chairs

get the 'Gustavian' treatment

To a contemporary eye the special appeal of furniture of the Gustavian period is its unstuffy, approachable blend of grandeur and homeliness. The grandeur, perhaps better defined as 'aristocratic' style, derives, however loosely, from the classic pieces made by Europe's leading cabinet-makers. The homeliness comes partly from the simplification process needed to translate such designs into softwood, partly from the charm lent by a painted finish which time and use have eroded to an attractive softness of colour and texture. In this context, I remember particularly well an illustration of a complicated chair design by the eighteenth-century English designer, Batty Langley, in a Swedish book on chairs. It was evidently intended to be executed in hardwood, but beside it was a colour illustration of a painted Swedish chair, made after Langley's pattern in softwood. The Swedish chair captures the spirit of the original; the chinoiserie fretwork on seat and back is reproduced almost unaltered and the proportions are very similar. The crisply carved ornament, however, has been suppressed, while the legs are sturdier and the chair has acquired a soft blue-green paint finish. Asked to choose between the two versions, many people today would pick the Swedish one. It is altogether prettier and one instinctively knows that, whereas the Langley polished hardwood chair would need living up to, the Swedish country cousin would fit in comfortably anywhere. The combination of a stripped-down classic shape with a muted paint finish is uniquely Scandinavian.

opposite

With its sturdy, generous shape and vivid yellow paintwork pleasantly eroded by time and use, this is a handsome example of the sort of chair to be found in 'herr-hard' or gentleman farms all over Sweden.

Nowadays, the fashion is to paint reproduction pieces in this style with semi-transparent paints to allow the wood grain to 'ghost' through. This translucent finish is then glazed over with a slightly darker shade to give it warmth and character. Attractive though this finish is, I am doubtful whether it is what the eighteenth-century painters would have used. On many antique painted chairs the upper coats of paint have worn away to reveal a white, chalky base. This is most likely to be gesso, the fine plastery substance used for centuries to coat raw wood because it allowed a finely burnished surface to be built up layer by layer, with much patient rubbing back with cuttlebone and other abrasives, well before the introduction of sandpaper. Another possibility, unthinkable in modern Scandinavia, where health and safety requirements are stringent, is lead white, used as an undercoat. Over this a tinted lead paint might have been applied as a top coat. The subtle erosion of the coloured paint surface is typical of lead paint, which is dense, durable, flexible but soft.

Lead paints are now a tantalizing closed-door, since they have been legislated out of the market except in very special conservationist situations. However, my thoughts about the nature of the old paints decided my choice of a tinted standard undercoat to paint the chair shown in this project. Undercoat has a chalky quality, not unlike that of lead paint, plus good coverage, necessary to paint out a grey and replace it with yellow. The yellow tinted with yellow ochre was too buttery for my taste. The finishing coats of shellac were a last minute inspiration, designed to strengthen and fire up the yellow paint, which it did very rapidly and effectively; so effectively, in fact, that I wonder whether this trick was not also part of the eighteenth-century painter's repertoire as a quick way of making a cheap earth pigment more exciting.

Step-by-step

Some time ago I bought a set of four 'Queen Anne-style' chairs in a tacky 'walnut' stained finish because they were cheap and because something about their high curved backs and bulging legs reminded me of chairs I had noticed on my Scandinavian trips. These, however, had all been painted, some grey, some red ochre, and many a light but warm yellow with a saffron spark to it. With their typical checked linen covers in red or blue and white, they looked sturdy but stylish in a totally Swedish way. It was a revelation how the first coat of colour – a pale grey – transformed my reproduction chairs. A couple of years later, though, I hankered for the sparky yellow, and this is what I chose to show here.

Sets of chairs like these do still turn up, reasonably priced, with detachable pad seats, which usually need some re-upholstery. The first step, if you are painting them, is to strip or sand the existing finish as close to the clean, bare wood as possible. French polish dissolves with an application of methylated spirit followed by a rubbing-down with wire wool. Old varnishes need varnish stripper. Almost certainly your 'walnut' will turn out to be a mongrelly assortment of pale softwoods, possibly beech or poplar, but certainly nothing special. Fill all holes and cracks before starting. This will turn out to be a fine set of Gustavian-style chairs once completed and well worth all the trouble.

1

Over the clean, sanded and filled surfaces, apply one coat of standard oil-based white undercoat. Allow to dry. Sand lightly. Re-coat if the result is patchy. Turn the chairs upside down to make sure that you cover all parts. Mix white undercoat with yellow powder or tube oil colour. Paint the chairs all over with this mixture. Allow them to dry, then sand lightly, dust down and re-coat. Two, even three, coats may be needed to achieve a solid, uniform shade. The rubbing down, when dry, compacts the paint layers and gives a tougher, more lasting finish. Chairs, especially, are subjected to constant wear and tear and require more thorough treatment than, say, lamp bases or occasional tables.

Materials Check-list

✦ Varnish stripper or methylated spirits
✦ Wire wool
✦ 500ml standard white undercoat
✦ Yellow ochre powder colour (Nutshell do a good one) or yellow ochre artists' oil tube colour
✦ White spirit
✦ 500ml each of orange shellac and white polish (bleached shellac)
✦ Methylated spirit
✦ Extra-soft wire wool
✦ Craig and Rose Luxine Glaze (smallest size)
✦ Tinting colours (Mars orange, red oxide and raw sienna in artists' oil tube colour)
✦ Brushes: one standard 2 in. (5cm) paint brush, one smaller brush for getting into cracks and corners, one 'glider' for applying shellac, and another for applying glaze and varnish
✦ Craig and Rose Extra Pale Dead Flat Varnish or Eggshell Varnish (500ml or nearest size) these are always useful.

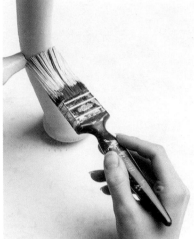

of a tint, mysteriously enriching the surface. Allow to dry for at least 24 hours.

4

The varnishing (with shellac) and glazing up to this point have been more for looks than strength. Now give your chairs two coats of either Craig and Rose Extra Pale Dead Flat or Eggshell Varnish for a serious protection, depending on whether you prefer a toally matt or mildly glossy finish which can be rubbed back later to dull it down.

Lastly, re-cover the padded seats with a vivid check fabric. In Sweden this would have been handwoven linen (flax-growing being a native industry), but cheaper imported Indian checked cottons have the same sort of robust charm and clear colouring.

2

To seal and make the paint less 'tender', as well as enhancing the colour, brush over two or three coats of shellac using a 50/50 mix of orange shellac or button polish and white (or bleached) polish (shellac), 'let down' or diluted with a splash of methylated spirit. Use a soft clean glider brush to apply the shellac and 'float' on the varnish copiously, smoothing it out quickly but without too much re-brushing, which creates streakiness. Don't hurry the drying time. Shellac feels touch-dry surprisingly fast – about half an hour – but hardens appreciably overnight. After the first coat is hard dry, rub down gingerly with fine grade (i.e. soft-to-handle) wire wool, just enough to even out any streakiness, dull the 'glitzy' shine and provide a key for the next coat. Repeat this operation once or twice. Each time you will find the bland, buttery paint shade taking on more depth and sparkle.

3

The bland yellow will now have acquired a warm saffron depth and a mildly shiny, smooth surface. Over this apply a thinned orange-red glaze, made up of Mars orange, red oxide and raw sienna (in proportions to taste) dissolved into white spirit and then mixed into an oil scumble, like Craig and Rose Luxine Glaze. Brush this on part by part, leave for a moment, then wipe off with a rag, to leave just the hint

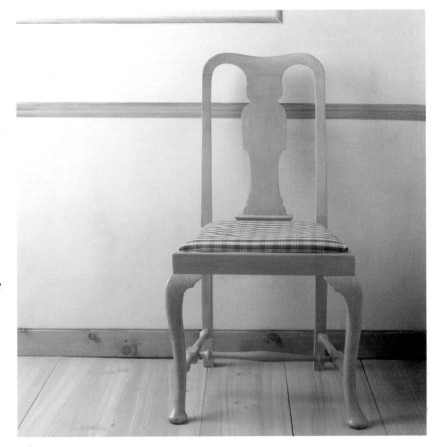

Gustavian Mirror

with gilded bow top-knot

One characteristic common to many wealthier Scandinavian interiors is a love of sparkling or reflective glass and crystal. Even quite modest homes have suitably scaled-down chandeliers or lustres. Mirrors, too, are everywhere, as they seem to have been since the eighteenth century. But whereas Venetian mirrors are murky and mysterious, their Nordic counterparts are bright and flashing and, as often as not, set off by rich gilding, a skill at which Swedish craftsmen in particular excelled. The reason for this crystalline display was always the need to increase and dramatize light, whether the brilliantly clear sunlight of the northern summers, or the spectral 'snow-light' of winter and early spring, or even the warm and romantic candlelight which heightens festive occasions, especially Christmas.

With electricity so readily to hand, we tend to forget how precious light – from candles, oil lamps or tapers – must have been to people living in near darkness through most of their working day during five months of the year. Fire-light and candle-light, especially, have a symbolic appeal to the Scandinavian temperament, even though there are obviously few homes now without electricity. The sight of a wavering flame in a window, seen through the darkness of the Scandinavian winter and dense forest, must have looked like a vivid promise of safety, warmth and human company to a traveller on skis or sleigh.

Mirror glass is a wonderfully effective means of magnifying candle-light. A lighted candle in front of a mirror gives a double light – the flame plus its reflection. This simple phenomenon led to a vogue for candelabra standing before pier-glasses, for mirror-backed wall sconces, for any means whereby the precious, dark-defeating flame could be redoubled and magnified.

The earlier Gustavian-style mirrors, dating from the mid eighteenth century, have the rounded or oval shape of the Rococo period. Later Neoclassical designs have rectangular frames, like the one shown in our project. A peculiarly Scandinavian feature of both styles is the pretty beribboned top-knot that appears on so many examples. The most lavish mirror frames were finished in water gilt, but a mixture of paint and gilding is also commonly found, as are entire finishes in chalky pastel colours, often with the carved details picked out in two or three colours. A typical colour scheme might be pale grey for the main frame, with the top-knot picked out in yellow ochre, pale blue and muted green.

opposite

Scandinavian painters/ craftsmen have always been exceptionally skilful and subtle in their use of gold leaf. There are few grand Scandinavian houses without the warm gleam of burnished water gilding on furniture or mirrors, as here.

left

An exceptionally attractive mirror-cum candle-holder from the Baroque period.

right

A water gilt mirror frame of the late Gustavian period, demonstrating the richness of pure gold leaf applied traditionally.

Step-by-step

Mirrors like these are a typical element in any Gustavian-style interior. Round or oval forms tend to belong to the earlier period, while rectangular shapes like this elegant pine reproduction are characteristic of the Neoclassical period, which extended well after King Gustav III's assassination in 1792 and is still enormously influential today.

Sometimes mirrors like these are wholly gilt. The method used would have been water-gilding over gesso and a tinted bole. There is a very strong tradition of gilding in Scandinavia, a Swedish variant of which is to combine a little gilding with soft, transparent paint finishes. This is the combination we have used here. For the transparent paint to look its best, the pine of the soft-wood base needs to be good-quality, free from knots and close grained. We used the much easier gilding method of applying transfer gold leaf over a new PVA-type size.

Materials Check-list

- ✦ Button polish
- ✦ Methylated spirit
- ✦ Glider brush for sealing
- ✦ Fine grade sandpaper
- ✦ Acrylic gesso
- ✦ Barn Red Woodwash
  (or Indian or Venetian Red acrylic)
- ✦ Wundasize
- ✦ One book of 23 carat transfer gold leaf
  (we used 12 out of 20 sheets)
- ✦ Fitch for tamping (optional)
- ✦ Two shades of green acrylic paint for frame, mid green and a darker green (made with Galeria pthalo blue, raw umber, yellow ochre)
- ✦ Craig and Rose Extra Pale Dead Flat Varnish (optional) or natural shoe polish
- ✦ Acrylic scumble glaze

1
The routine shellac treatment should be given to the wood, followed by sanding, to seal and smooth it. The bow top-knot was given three coats of acrylic gesso, rubbed smooth in between coats when dry. This creates a smooth poreless base for the gilding to shine out properly.

2

The gesso was sealed with shellac and allowed to dry before the application of a coat of Barn Red Woodwash which approximates to the red bole (clayey) base used in water gilding.

3

A grey-green acrylic paint was then mixed – a coffee-cupful is enough – using pthalo blue, yellow ochre and raw umber acrylic colours mixed with a little white emulsion. This was brushed thinly over the whole frame, bar the bow, so the wood grain showed through.

4

A darker version of the same green was made by adding a touch more blue and raw umber to the previous mixture. This was brushed over the 'bead' or 'pearl' moulding on the inside edge of the frame next to the glass. The glass was protected with masking tape to save time later when cleaning up.

5

When the red paint on the bow was dry, a coat of Wundasize was brushed over the whole bow as evenly as possible. It looks milky at first but rapidly goes clear. It is ready to gild after 20-30 minutes.

6

Gilding is done by laying sheets of wax-paper-backed transfer gold leaf gold side down on the size and slightly overlapping. Pressing firmly with your fingers or 'pouncing' with a solid fitch as here, push the gold leaf down on to the tacky size, to which it instantly adheres. Peel off the wax-paper backing and continue until as much of the surface as possible (minus maybe a few inaccessible undercut bits) is gilded.

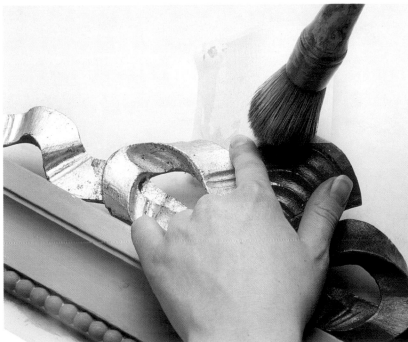

7

Where gaps occur, simply press down a scrap of leftover leaf. Leave the leaf to 'set up' for several hours or overnight, then go over it all with a soft brush, smoothing it down and clearing off loose 'skewings'. Any remaining gaps can be touched in with yellow ochre paint if they are obtrusive, or gilt cream as here.

8

A little acrylic scumble glaze with raw umber was brushed over the paler green frame and then wiped off with tissue after a minute or two, to soften and 'shade' the colour slightly. The mirror frame can be varnished with a clear matt varnish (not the gilding), but in our view this is not necessary here, since frames get little wear. For a quick finish that can be polished, try clear wax polish or shoe polish.

Bedside Cupboard
decorated with 'stänkmålning' (spatter painting)

Spatter painting is such a widely practised traditional paint effect in Sweden that there is a special name for it, 'stänkmålning', pronounced 'shtenkmawlning'. It is not a furniture finish, strictly speaking, and is found most frequently on the dado section of walls, where it imitates natural granite. It makes a practical but impressive finish which can be highly varnished, making it durable and easy to keep clean. This type of 'stänkmålning' is seen in the foyers to buildings with some pretensions, such as banks, offices or the solid town-houses of the nineteenth-century bourgeoisie. There is an especially refined version of grey-granite spatter painting in the dining room of the Haga Pavilion, the exquisite summer pavilion built on the outskirts of Stockholm by King Gustav III in the latter half of the eighteenth century.

Less elegant, but more spirited, is the use made of spatter painting in Scandinavian country homes and cottages, where the intention seems to have been to create an all-over pattern imitating wallpaper in cheerful and appealing colours. A modest 'stuga' may have walls painted a warm brick-red (indoor cousin to the iron-oxide-based Falun Red used on the vast majority of painted wooden exteriors in Sweden), with bold spattering in white. This looks handsome and heart-warming in a rough, rustic style and makes a cheerful background to painted furniture and bare scrubbed floors. Another, more elaborate, version features random swathes of spatters in red, dark blue and white on a warm yellow ochre ground. Here the intention is clearly to imitate wallpaper, but to modern eyes it more closely resembles action-painting.

opposite
Spatter painting, or 'stänkmålning' is usually deployed as here on walls, especially below the dado. Note the 'all-over' stencil imitating wallpaper above.

Traditionally 'stänkmålning' was done with bundles of fine, whippy birch twigs rather than brushes, and the paint used was 'soft' distemper, or one of the closely related casein-bound paints, both of which produce a chalky, blotting-paper texture. This combination must have resulted from trial and error, since it undoubtedly produces the best results. The birch twigs throw off freckles of colour which are more open and distinct than those projected from a brush, while the blotting-paper texture of the water-based base paint is absorbent enough to fix the flying spots of wet colour rapidly, making them less likely to splatter and then run down. The painter would spatter one colour at a time, using a different bundle of twigs for each colour. The prescribed method for applying the paint is something like an underarm tennis serve from a standing position well back from the wall surface, though for more even, close spatters the painter would move in closer. Some colour is bound to get on to the floor and ceiling, so the ceiling would have been painted out afterwards and the floor well protected by dust sheets or possibly, in really remote areas, comon straw.

The charm of this cheap and cheerful finish is that it can produce beguilingly rich and colourful textures speedily, and these can be colour-keyed to other elements of an interior by using a combination of colours already present. I have used 'stänkmålning' to soften and cool off a distempered wall colour which looked like pale coral in the tin and dried to a vivid smoked-salmon orange. Usually distempers dry much paler, so this was an unexpected problem. Spattering in white, grey and black failed to 'knock back' the overheated effect. It was not until I had worked out that green, as the complementary colour to red, was the missing 'neutralising' element that the overall effect settled down satisfactorily.

Step-by-step

This little 'pot cupboard' comes from a range of high-quality pine reproductions of Gustavian furniture; it has the straight, tapered legs typical of the Neo-classical style. The corrugated surface of the doors is a decorative touch popular with Swedish joiners and is seen on peasant furniture as well as more upmarket pieces. I liked the idea of using the 'stänkmålning' finish on furniture, even though it is most often used as a finish for walls. This particular colour scheme of white, grey and gunmetal on a pale, cool pink, inspired by a modern Swedish wallpaper design, seemed ideal for a bedroom piece. Water-based paint was used throughout for speed, but also to provide the absorbent surface suited to spattering.

Materials Check-list

- ✦ Standard orange shellac
- ✦ 500ml standard white matt emulsion
- ✦ Nutshell red oxide powder pigment
- ✦ Raw umber and lamp-black gouache
- ✦ Standard 2 in. (5cm) decorating brush
- ✦ Bundle of 'stänkmålning' birch twigs or standard brush
- ✦ Craig and Rose Extra Pale Dead Flat Varnish or Matt Acrylic Varnish
- ✦ Fine sable brush for 'beauty spots' (optional)
- ✦ Yoghurt pots for colours
- ✦ Rags
- ✦ Fine sandpaper or fine wire wool
- ✦ Paper tissues or kitchen roll for mopping up trickles

1

A little red oxide powder pigment with water and rather less raw umber were mixed into standard white emulsion to make a pale greyish pink. This was used to base-coat the cupboard, which had previously been given two coats of shellac, rubbed down with fine sandpaper to seal knots and prevent the wood soaking up too much paint. Two coats were needed, again rubbed back lightly when dry.

2

Small quantities – approximately 200ml – of spatter colours were prepared, using plain white emulsion, greyed with raw umber, and the previous mixture darkened with black gouache and a little water. We used the traditional birch-twig bundle for the spattering, because it gives more random, larger dots. But with a little practice, a standard paint-brush can be an effective substitute. In both cases the tips of the twigs or bristles are dipped into the spatter colour, which should be quite fluid, but with a 'milk' rather than a 'water' consistency. The painting hand is jogged on the other wrist to send spots of wet paint flying. A little practice is needed to get the spatter consistency right – too wet and it trickles – and to get one's aim under control. Use paper or a

sheet of card to practice on. Position a ground-sheet or newspaper behind the piece to catch any stray paint. We found it best to prop the piece up on a slight slant. Keep tissues handy to mop up any odd trickle at once.

3

The white spatter goes on first, randomly and lightly. This operation is repeated on all surfaces, one at a time. The spatters dry almost immediately, so this is less time-consuming than it sounds.

4

Next, the mid-grey spatters are added in exactly the same way. To spatter the inside legs, the piece was turned on its head.

5

Lastly, the black or near-black was applied. In the original design these spots were sparse but larger, a difficult effect to achieve using the traditional method. So you can either go for blackish spots on the same scale as the others, using the method described, or add larger black 'beauty spots' by hand with a watercolour brush.

6

Finish off by giving the entire piece two coats of either Craig and Rose Extra Pale Dead Flat Varnish (oil-based) or Matt Acrylic Varnish, which is faster drying and non-yellowing, but slightly less durable. Smooth each coat of varnish when dry with fine abrasive paper or fine wire wool, brushing down well each time. Do not scour the varnish, but just apply enough pressure to clear away any grit, etc., which may have settled on the drying varnish.

N.B. The insides of painted pieces should be painted too, especially the backs of doors. Such surfaces can be left pink, without spattering. Varnish inside, though, as a protection against dust and spills.

Betrothal Box

with Rococo rose decoration

Pretty caskets and boxes like the one shown here are among the most appealing, and collected, examples of early peasant art. This example may well have been a 'betrothal box', presented by a young man to his fiancée as a love token. The date and initials suggest that it was intended to record a special occasion, while the gaiety of its colouring and design show that it must have been destined to please a female heart. The young man in question would have had to weigh up the financial considerations, because this box is the work of a 'named' artist, Mattias Hansson, who worked in the western part of the province of Dalarna. It is significant perhaps that the box has a lock; a young woman could stow her love letters and trinkets safely in her own locked box. One suspects that privacy must have been cherished in a peasant society where so many people lived, slept and worked in one or two rooms.

Other examples of work by the same artist can be seen in the Dalarnas Museum and they indicate that he was something of an innovator, both in his choice of colouring and his feeling for design. The brightness of his palette is interesting in that it was around the eighteen-forties, that commercial use of aniline colours, chemically produced, introduced a rush of brilliant colour into European textiles, wallpapers and – gradually – pigments. One suspects that the painter was aware of these changes and that he had also taken note of the vividness and smartness of a style of decoration prevalent in the early nineteenth century,

loosely influenced by the Neoclassical movement. This style had been radically affected by the late eighteenth-century archaeological discoveries at Pompeii. In England this was called 'Regency', in France 'Empire' and in Germany 'Biedermeier'. It was characterized by rectilinear designs – in contrast to the curves of Rococo – by the use of strong contrasts, like black, with red or green, as in this example, and by a liberal use of gold or gilding. In peasant terms this would be modified to suit the market, so gold becomes ochre-yellow (a traditional substitute) and the typical palette is more vivid (orange-red or vermilion instead of brown-red). The whole is counterpointed by a sophisticated use of black. Black, however, needs enlivening, as Hansson recognized, by neat and perky decoration if it is not to become sombre. He used the carved stamps which survive still in basket decoration, for their ease and speed of use, one would guess, and also because of their 'chic'.

Our lap-desk, or 'writing slope' as it was and still is known in antiquarian circles, invited a somewhat different scheme of decoration, more Rococo than Neoclassical and more pretty than 'chic'. I would certainly like to know what Mattias Hansson would have done with such inviting surfaces.

opposite
Scandinavian peasant painters seem to have found painting boxes especially congenial.

right

The sophisticated colouring of this betrothal box by Mattias Hansson mark it out as an early nineteenth-century piece even without the date.

Step-by-step

Our 'betrothal box' is actually a low-priced, softwood 'blank' made in California where it is known as a 'lap desk'. But the shape is so reminiscent of the decorated writing boxes Swedish young men used to present to their fiancées as betrothal gifts that it is tempting to wonder whether the Californian maker had some Swedish maternal ancestor who brought her treasured memento with her on the journey to a new life in the New World. Californian softwood, however, is knottier and less dense and weighty than Scandinavian pine, so our box required filling, sanding and three coats of sealer before it could be decorated with this pretty, muted, Gustavian-style design.

Materials Check-list

- ✦ Button shellac
- ✦ Glider brush
- ✦ Methylated spirit to clean brush
- ✦ Fine filler
- ✦ Fine grade sandpaper
- ✦ Gustavian Green Woodwash, sample-jar size
- ✦ Olive Green Woodwash, sample-jar size
- ✦ White Aquarelleable pencil
- ✦ Liquitex Flow Enhancer
- ✦ Two or three sable watercolour brushes
- ✦ Burnt sienna, Windsor blue, ochre, white, black, raw umber acrylic colours for decoration
- ✦ Acrylic scumble glaze
- ✦ Craig and Rose Extra Pale Dead Flat Varnish
- ✦ Rags
- ✦ Saucers, etc.

1

Cracks were filled with fine surface filler and rubbed down, as was the bristly end grain. Three coats of button shellac were applied, rubbed down lightly between coats once they had become hard to seal off knots and give a less absorbent finish generally. Two coats of Gustavian Green Woodwash, a fast drying acrylic paint, were brushed over the surface, thinned with a little water each time for smoothness, then rubbed back lightly when dry with fine sandpaper each time.

2

A watery solution of Olive Green Woodwash was brushed fairly evenly over the Gustavian Green base. This gives a beautiful, subtle, glaucous shade, like frosted bottle glass.

3

When dry, the design was sketched out freehand with white Aquarelleable pencil. Using fine watercolour brushes and dull red, blue-grey, pale cream and grey acrylics for the flowers, and raw umber with a dot of black for the foliage and bows (all with Flow Enhancer), the sketched roses, leaves and fluttering ribbons were painted over.

4

Using a glaze made up of acrylic scumble tinted with raw umber acrylic and thinned with a little water, a darkening glaze was brushed over the whole box, decoration included.

5

The glaze was then rubbed off with a rag here and there to soften the effect.

6

Two coats of Craig and Rose Extra Pale Dead Flat Varnish were finally brushed over the whole box, inside and out and rubbed down when dry, until the box felt agreeable to hold. This is always a point to remember in the case of small pieces which will be held and handled frequently.

N.B. Our box was painted a dull red inside for contrast, but you might prefer to paper it with a small sprig or marbled paper.

Long Wall Cupboard

with distressed finish and 'kurbits' decoration

Ask any Swede to name something quintessentially Swedish in folk painting and the odds are that the answer will be 'kurbits' painting. This style of decoration, immediately recognizable, originated in the central province of Dalarna, north of Stockholm, in the last decades of the eighteenth century. The distinctive feature of a 'kurbits' painting is a cluster of outsize flower heads rocketing upwards and outwards, dwarfing houses, church spires or riders on horseback. Peasant art freely uses flower motifs to crowd colour into the interstices of mural paintings. These 'kurbits' motifs, however, in all their exuberant, overarching enormity, do contribute a surreal dimension to what are, typically, scenes illustrating Bible stories, where all the protagonists are shown dressed in contemporary Swedish costume against the backdrop of a village, mill or workshop.

The accepted theory about the origins of these motifs is that they derive from the gourd vine ('cucurbita') which the Lord caused to sprout in the desert to protect Jonah from the heat of the noonday sun. Anyone who has grown courgettes or marrows will recognize something of their monstrous energy in the 'kurbits' motifs. Posies run wild and proliferate in a slightly menacing way over domestic and Biblical scenes in this curious variant of Swedish peasant art.

The 'kurbits' paintings of Dalarna are generally attributed to two schools, Rattvik or Leksand. Unusually, in an area where so much work is anonymous, over forty painters in each school are known by name and their individual styles documented. Sometimes they signed their work instead of incorporating the names and dates of the clients for whom a piece was destined, which was the more usual practice.

While the highlights of 'kurbits' painting were undoubtedly the odd, humorous, naïve wall paintings executed on that other peculiarly Swedish institution, the 'party' house, it was not long before 'kurbits' painters were decorating furniture in this distinctive style. The Rattvik school, especially, painted and sold furniture ornamented with 'kurbits' motifs. The rocketing blooms or bouquets usually stand alone on such pieces usefully filling tall, narrow panels on cupboard doors, clock-cases, or built-in cupboard beds. Here, the style varies with the painter, but typically, the soaring 'kurbits' bouquet is highly schematized, almost abstract, in its upward geometry of symmetrical shapes which gradually dwindle to a point, like a highly idiosyncratic piece of topiary in colour. The Rattvik school adopted a low-toned palette for such work, using a lot of brown, some red, cream or dull green against a prevailing background of blue black, which would sometimes be enlivened by another regional speciality, the 'clouds marbling' of the adjacent province of Hålsingland. The combination of these two techniques is highly effective – the rich muted colours of the 'kurbits' decoration, provides an attractive counterpoint to the sprightly arabesques of the 'clouds marbling', the pale scallops against a background shade of thundery blue.

Sometimes, too, the background was enriched by some hand graining, using vinegar or beer glazes. These were 'stamped' while wet with the side of the bunched hand to create 'sausage' shapes which were used adroitly to imitate – loosely – the upmarket fashion for edging drawers, clock-cases and other pieces of furniture with radially figured veneer.

opposite
Colourful wall paintings in the Kurbits style would be used to dress up a room and transform it into party mood. The example shown here is of exceptional quality.

Step-by-step

The old cupboard treated here was actually found in a skip; it looked as though it must have been in a hospital originally, since it bore the painted inscription "Poison Cupboard". It had been painted once before, but this time I felt it would look well with a dark-blue, distressed finish overall, but with the front panel painted a deep red and embellished with the lively traditional 'kurbits' style motif (see p.151 for a 'kurbits' elongated flower bouquet and vase to copy or adapt). The inside of the cupboard was to be left red and unimproved; it was felt that its slightly battered look added character.

Materials Check-list

- ✦ Fine sandpaper
- ✦ Medium grade wire wool
- ✦ 500ml each Barn Red, Olive and Midnight Woodwash (or similar acrylic colours)
- ✦ Household wax candle
- ✦ Aquarelleable white pencil for outlining design
- ✦ Masking tape (optional)
- ✦ Standard brush for applying Woodwash
- ✦ Selection of watercolour brushes for 'kurbits' motif
- ✦ Assorted colours for decoration (bearing in mind that both the Olive and Midnight can be used 'straight' or lightened with white emulsion
- ✦ Black tube acrylic
- ✦ Liquitex Flow Enhancer
- ✦ Raw umber tube acrylic
- ✦ Acrylic scumble
- ✦ Acrylic matt varnish

1

After a good clean inside and out, followed by sanding (kitchen cupboards tend to collect the remains of foodstuffs as well as greasy fingerprints) the main body of the exterior was painted with Olive Green Woodwash and the front panel with Barn Red Woodwash. Both paints were then allowed to dry for approximately half an hour.

2
Only the green areas are to be distressed, allowing some green to 'surface' through the Midnight Woodwash top coat. To achieve this distressed effect quickly and easily, rub a plain wax candle quite firmly over the paintwork, as shown. The wax deposited should be thick enough to show clearly. Too much wax is better than too little.

3
A coat of Midnight is added over the whole of the green waxed paint in sufficient quantity to cover it entirely. The red panel can be masked off with tape if you like. When dry, rub down the Midnight (or whatever colour) top coat with medium wire wool in the direction of the wood grain. You will find the green beneath will show through clearly and naturally. Carry on over the whole piece.

4

Using the white Aquarelleable pencil, the 'kurbits' motif (see p.151) is sketched in, extended to fill the panel space. The shapes are then painted in with various sizes of watercolour brush in strong, simple colours. Those here were chosen to show up against the red-brown base – yellow ochre, deep green, chalky-blue, creamy-white and black. Practise with a fine sable brush (Pro Arte Size 4) and add a little Flow Enhancer to the black outlining colour to achieve the bouncy, full curves shown here and the fine flicks at the tip of leaf shapes.

5

When the decoration is dry, brush a 'dirty' antiquing glaze over it (we used raw umber acrylic in a little acrylic scumble), wiping back with a soft rag to lighten some areas a shade more than others. Allow the glaze to dry. Varnish the cupboard inside and out with – for speed – two coats of matt acrylic varnish; each coat dries in approximately 20 minutes and it is non-yellowing.

Japanned Desk

with chinoiserie decoration

Chinoiserie, that whimsically sophisticated style of decoration in which western Rococo flirted with the mysterious Orient, appeared in Scandinavia some decades later than in the rest of Europe. When it did arrive, however, in the shape of a delicious Chinese pavilion built by the Swedish king as a thirty-fourth-birthday present for his German wife, Louisa Ulrike, it took the Swedish court by storm. The original wooden pavilion, unveiled in 1753, is described in a letter from the queen to her mother: 'There was a main room decorated in Indian style with four big porcelain vases, one in each corner. In the other rooms there were old Japanese lacquer cabinets and sofas covered with Indian fabrics, all in the finest taste. There was a bedchamber with Indian fabrics on the walls and bed, and the walls were decorated with the finest porcelain, pagodas, vases and birds.

As this quotation suggests, Scandinavia was as confused about the provenance of 'chinoiserie' as the rest of Europe had been since the first examples of Chinese lacquer, porcelain and Indian painted 'chintses' had begun to reach its shores a century or more earlier. Few Europeans had actually been to such remote places and travellers' tales were extravagant. The easiest solution was to imagine that all these charming, covetable treasures came from Cathay, a half imaginary legendary territory just beyond the known world of trade, where 'big porcelain vases' (almost certainly Chinese rather than Japanese), pagodas, porcelain and Indian fabrics reflected a fairy-tale exoticism whose strangeness stirred the imagination but whose real geographical boundaries hardly mattered.

The pavilion lasted only ten years in its original light-hearted wooden form. In 1763, the court architect, Carl-Frederick Adelcrantz, replaced it with a more solid, brick-built version on the same spot, which is the 'Kina' that still stands today in the grounds of the palace of Drottningholm. The Swedish royal family adored it, treating it as their own version of the Petit Trianon at Versailles, a private retreat where they could escape from protocol. There, ' the king worked with his lathe, the queen listened to her reader, the prince drew, the princesses made lace, Prince Carl sailed his frigate, Prince Frederick ran about on the grass and the guards smoked their pipes'.

The Adelcrantz Kina Pavilion may seem a touch austere at first sight. The Indian chintzes, porcelain jars and Japanese cabinets, have been removed, perhaps to other royal residences. But what remains is striking and excellent of its kind: many-windowed chambers painted green and gold, blue, yellow and red, the brilliant colours further decorated with vivid 'chinoiserie' scenes in the much emulated style of Boucher and Pillement.

Not many people would be tempted to decorate whole rooms in the 'chinoiserie' style today, but as a finish for a special item of furniture it is well within the scope of a moderately experienced decorative painter. Copy or adapt designs of the period just as the early painters did. Unlike true Oriental lacquer, which has a restricted palette, 'japanning' was executed in a wide range of shades, including coromandel red, vermilion, lapis-blue, jonquil-yellow, cream, green and, of course, a great deal of black. Remember that the many coats of yellowish shellac will change your base colour considerably. It will also 'knock back' the gold decoration.

opposite
This 'chinoiserie' wallpaper in Sweden's Drottningholm State Theatre epitomizes the quirky charm which made Oriental designs so irresistible to the eighteenth-century European aristocracy.

Step-by-step

One of the discoveries I made while working on this book is that a stylish paint treatment is the ideal disguise for repro pieces in the Queen Anne mode which have seen better days. Much repro furniture is ruined by its inferior finish, often a sticky-looking dark walnut stain and French polish. Conversely, the shape and proportions, modelled on distinguished forebears, are often pleasing. A paint finish, simple as in the case of the chair on p.113, or considerably more elaborate as here, covers up poor finish and mediocre work-manship, while focusing attention on the good basic structure.

The small flap-top desk shown here was a pave-ment bargain spotted outside a south London junk shop. The veneer was chipped here and there and a coat of grey paint had been slapped on in an attempt to mask the damage. The leather lining to the flap had disappeared and the interior pigeon-holes were of ordinary plywood, crudely varnished. But the size and shape were appealing and the drawers had unexpectedly handsome brass handles. I felt it would be an excellent subject for the raised, gilded chinoiserie decoration which I have been developing in studio classes.

The technique combines old and new: a fast drying acrylic modelling compound for raised elements in the chinoiserie motifs, plus a new acrylic gold paint for the 'gilding', but with a return to eighteenth-century practice in the many coats of orange shellac or button polish which complete the finish. Carefully rubbed back this tones down the garishness of the gold paint, while adding the interesting patina which is nine-tenths of the charm of a japanned piece. Experience has shown that cheap gold paint is indistinguishable from gold leaf once buried under many coats of shellac.

Materials Check-list

- ✦ Coarse, medium and fine grades of sandpaper
- ✦ Plastic wood for filling
- ✦ 1 litre flat oil paint in Slate from my Historic Range
- ✦ 500ml brown-red flat oil paint for the desk interior
- ✦ Standard paint brushes
- ✦ White spirit
- ✦ White Aquarelleable pencil
- ✦ Tracing paper (see p.153 for motifs)
- ✦ Acrylic modelling compound
- ✦ Red-brown acrylic for base coating raised work
- ✦ A selection of sable brushes from whisker fine to medium
- ✦ Pointed steel nail file or penknife
- ✦ Scalpel for whittling
- ✦ Gold acrylic paint from Paint Magic
- ✦ Nanking Encre de Chine by Le Franc Bourgeois
- ✦ Wundasize
- ✦ Light gold metallic powder
- ✦ 500ml white polish
- ✦ 500ml button polish
- ✦ Methylated spirit
- ✦ Craig and Rose Eggshell Varnish (optional)
- ✦ Rottenstone powder
- ✦ Rags
- ✦ Small saucers for paints

1

The desk was prepared first with a thorough sanding, filling (I used plastic wood) cracks and chips, followed by two coats of flat oil paint in a colour we call 'slate'. Water-based paint does not work well on veneered furniture as the water content is apt to loosen veneer. Step 1 shows a chinoiserie motif being traced on to the green base, using tracing paper which has been scribbled over on the back with white pencil. This leaves a faint but clear outline which is firmed up with the white pencil. This can be washed off where it is not wanted.

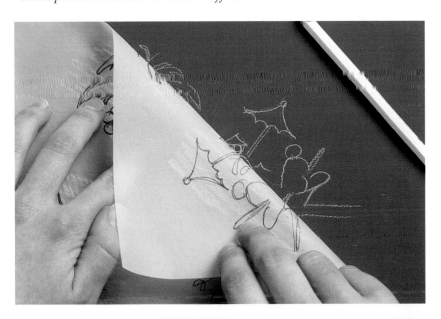

2

Several layers of acrylic modelling compound, softened in a little water and applied with a soft watercolour brush, are then put on to 'raise' areas of the design. These layers are built up like a contour map to make a rounded or domed shape. Simple shapes are best for this 'raised' work, here the palm trunk, boat and passengers. The compound dries very hard, so is best shaped with ad hoc tools like a pointed metal nail file, while it is still just pliable. When dry, it can be whittled with a sharp scalpel. Finally, it should be smoothed by rubbing carefully with sandpaper folded into small points to avoid damaging the base paint.

3

The main design elements are then painted in, including 'raised' work, with a red-brown (i.e. Venetian or Indian red) acrylic paint and soft watercolour brushes. This simulates the red bole, a clay base used in water gilding, which will later show through the gold paint here and there to give warmth and texture.

4

Acrylic gold paint and fine brushes are used to cover all the red areas, and to add extra detail to balance the motif. Double up the gold here and there for brilliance.

5

On old japanned pieces the gilded areas were drawn over and details added with fine black line work. I used a whisker-fine sable brush and Encre de Chine, as favoured by restorers, for this detailing. This must be left for 24 hours to harden before coating with shellac, otherwise the black lines will smudge.

6

Three coats of our standard shellac mixture – 50/50 button polish and white polish plus a splash of methylated spirit – were applied to seal and strengthen the decoration. The shellac was 'floated' on, using a soft brush, brushing each coat at right angles to the previous one and allowing

the shellac to harden thoroughly in between. The whole surface was then rubbed back gently but firmly, using fine wire wool in a circular polishing motion. This smoothes the surfaces, while slightly abrading the gold paint to let the red base show through on the raised areas.

7

After thorough dusting down, Wundasize was brushed on around the motif wherever a dusting of gold metallic powder was to be applied. After a few practice runs on paper, a soft medium sable was dipped into the gold powder and tapped gently to release a dusting of gold on to the size, which had been left to harden for 30 minutes. Try not to overdo the gold powdering, it should look cloudy, not solid.

8

After an overnight break to let the size harden properly, any excess gold powder can be brushed off. Several more coats of the shellac mixture detailed above were applied, criss-crossed and rubbed back as before. I had reached ten coats by the time this photograph was taken. Note how the yellow-brown shade of the shellac has changed the original slate colour to a convincingly eighteenth-century drab olive, while at the same time integrating the raised gilt decoration and gold powder dusting into the overall look of the piece. All the rawness of the contrasting elements is softened and 'knocked back', so the decoration is seen as incidental to the overall effect rather than as a series of islands of brightness against a dark ground. It may seem perverse to spend time working up decorative elements only to subdue them deliberately again, but the old japanners knew what they were doing, taking the long way round to achieve the best result, an effect of subtle enrichment rather than a 'razzle-dazzle' one which quickly palls. A further advantage of the japanning finish is the deliciously fine, deep gloss created by layers of thin spirit varnish, finely abraded.

N.B. The correct way to apply shellac is with a charged brush, starting in the middle and brushing out fast to left and right. Try not to overbrush to avoid streakiness, though rubbing back will help even this out.

9

Lastly, since shellac is not alcohol- or water-proof, it may be advisable to finish off with a thinned coat of a tougher oil-based alkyd varnish like Craig and Rose Eggshell Varnish. This should be rubbed to dim the shininess and then polished to the requisite soft lustre with a paste of rottenstone in water rubbed on gently with a cloth pad, then wiped off with a damp cloth. Finally buff up with a soft clean cloth.

Motifs

Recipes

for making traditional Scandinavian paints

Olgefarg/oil paint

This is a lean oil paint for use on woodwork or furniture under oil or tempera paint. It is rendered more transparent by adding further white spirit, and more opaque by increasing the ratio of zinc white. Traditionally, the coats moved from thin (less oil) to fat (more oil), and many thin coats were preferred to fewer thick ones.

Ingredients
1 kg zinc white pigment
4 decilitres boiled linseed oil
3 decilitres white spirit
5 centilitres dryers or siccative (obtainable from artists' suppliers)

To mix, place 1 decilitre of oil in a bucket, mix in the powder pigment until dissolved, then add alternatively oil, white spirit and dryers, stirring thoroughly. For successive coats moderately increase the quantity of oil each time. These will take longer to dry, but give a smoother, low lustre finish with greater protective power. Varnish is rarely used in Scandinavia.

All-purpose white undercoat/primer

This would be applied under oil paint or under egg tempera where solid, opaque colour was required. Under dark colours it would be tinted, possibly using a cheaper pigment.

Ingredients
1 kg zinc white
7 decilitres boiled linseed oil
10 decilitres white spirit
pigment (optional) dissolved in oil or white spirit

Make a paste from half the oil plus all the zinc white, then add, mixing thoroughly, the rest of the oil and the white spirit. This gives a sloppy, semi-transparent white base with sufficient 'tooth' to grip the subsequent paint.

Limfarg/Distemper

Pronounced 'limfay', this formula gives a soft distemper with a powdery bloom. The better the size used the less tendency it has to rub off. Rabbit-skin glue is of superior strength. By adding dry powder pigment dissolved in water, beautiful, clear pastel shades can be obtained. Limfarg can be painted over an existing emulsion, but not the other way round. To overpaint distemper use a weaker – i.e. less size – mix of distemper. It is applied with a large, not too soft brush in a cross-hatching style, and gives good coverage – one coat is enough.

Ingredients
5 kg chalk or whiting
1.5 decilitres rabbit-skin glue
1 ten-litre bucket and one smaller bucket
large wooden spoons for stirring
dry powder pigment for tinting

Put 2½ litres of water into a 10 litre bucket, add the chalk or whiting, pouring until a cone forms above the water. Leave overnight to absorb water and 'fatten' as painters say.

In the small bucket put 1.5 decilitres of rabbit-skin granules with enough water to cover and leave overnight.

The next day set the glue to heat slowly in a bain marie, and when melted – do not bring to boil – without lumps, stir into the chalk/water mixture, mixing vigorously until thoroughly amalgamated. This mixture gives a warm white. To tint add dissolved powder colour, again stirring thoroughly. It is important to see the powder pigment is well-dissolved. Distemper dries several shades lighter, so it may be sensible to test colour on a card, drying with a hair-dryer, to check the final shade.

Organic glazes

The thin malleable glazes used so commonly in Scandinavian furniture painting can be made from flat ale, vinegar, buttermilk or whey, or PVA diluted with water. To all of these add dry powder pigment, mixing well, and test on cards for colour intensity and adhesion.

Shellac

The cheapest form of shellac (worthwhile if you are using it copiously) is made by dissolving flake shellac in methylated spirit. Leave the flakes to soak and dissolve over several days in methylated spirits. Stir well and test on card. For greater fluidity — needed over large surfaces – add more methylated spirit. Apply with a sharp soft brush – fine bristles are necessary – in the centre of a surface, brushing out fast to left and right. Overbrush as little as possible.

Composition putty or compo

This is a traditional mixture used to create 'raised' decoration and for filling cracks and blemishes.

Mix equal parts of boiled linseed oil, bread flour, chalk or whiting with quarter part of damar varnish or resin. It is easiest to combine these smoothly if they are all kept at the same temperature.

Egg/oil tempera

This is a thin paint, slow drying but of astonishing toughness which was often used in the eighteenth century as a ground for decorative painting on furniture. It is most suited to pale shades. It takes a week to dry, but continues drying and hardening indefinitely. When dry it can be buffed to a fine sheen. The ground should be the 'all-purpose white undercoat' detailed on the opposite page, left for 24 hours before over painting with egg/oil tempera.

Ingredients
egg yolks, the fresher the better
boiled linseed oil
water
white spirit
pigment

To make: mix 1 part egg yolk with 1 part boiled linseed oil and 2 parts water (some people use distilled water), add a few drops of white spirit, and store in the fridge. When needed, sieve the mixture through muslin or old tights to remove any skin, then add the pigment. For greater opacity use more pigment. For a semi-transparent glaze use more oil and water. Shake well in a jar with a tight lid to emulsify well before use. Drying time varies between 3-7 days depending on climate and humidity.

Glossary

ALMOGE Folk, all people literally.

BARNASKORNA Swedish for special baskets.

BAUERNMALEREI The Austrian/German variation on folk art, with roses, flowers etc.

BIEDERMEIER is the German/Austrian name for a typically bourgeois nineteenth-century style of decoration/furnishing which is now much collected and imitated: Neoclassical meets the nineteenth century High Street!

BIRCH GRAINING Paint effects imitative of Scandinavia's most prolific wood – distinctive for its curving patterns and blond colouring.

BRIDE OF ÅNGERMANLAND The name given to a particular Rococo style of long-case clock made and decorated in this most northern Swedish province; imitating the wedding regalia or costume of a typical local bride – head-dress, belt, necklace, purse, etc.

CASEIN A milk or cheese derivative, acts as a binder in many old local paints but is now thoroughly a part of modern paint chemistry – tough, durable and cheap.

CLOUDS MARBLING A naïve or folk or peasant nineteenth-century style of marbling in paint characteristic of Dalarna and other more northerly Swedish provinces. Unlike marble – blue, for starters – but decorative in itself and instantly recognizable.

ENGLISH RED The name given in Scandinavia to a softer, purer form of iron-oxide red, a spin-off of iron mining.

FALUN ROT Swedish name for a local iron-oxide red paint used on exteriors from the mid nineteenth century based on casein with the local brown-red pigment.

FARMER MARBLING See CLOUDS MARBLING – a naïve style of marble imitation which can be more or less like the real thing depending on the background and knowledge of the painter.

FAUX MARBRE A much used term, especially in the United States, for 'imitation marble' painting. 'Faux' means 'false' or 'fake'.

FITCH Hog – bristle brush with sturdy enough bristles to help colour mixing by dispensing pure colour in solvent quickly and effectively as a standard paint brush it retains colour extremely well.

GUSTAVIANSK The adjective formed from the name of Gustav III of Sweden to describe the cool, Neoclassical pastel style of decoration associated with his reign.

JAPANNING The European craftsman's answer to real Oriental lacquer; using many coats of shellac to build up a glossy and deep finish on painted, often gilded and decorated furniture. Technically quite different but looks similar – i.e. rich and shiny. Not so durable – true lacquer was used in Japan for Samurai armour!

KISTA Swedish for 'chest', which can be small or large but is essentially a box of wood painted and decorated, sometimes carved too.

KURBITS A freakish and regional style of decorative painting in Dalarna, Sweden, said to derive 'name-wise' from the vine the Lord caused to grow up and shelter the prophet Jonal in the mid-day desert heat.

MARMORERING Simply Swedish for 'marbling', i.e. imitating the veins and incidents of the natural stone with paint.

MDF The latest wood substitute – wood sawdust bound with various resins – very smooth, heavy, takes 'routing' well. Not allowed in the United States for dust/fall-out reasons.

MORA-KLOCKA A celebrated school or workshop making long case and other clocks for the Scandinavian peasantry from approximately 1780 to 1850. Much decorated, but the round in late lace is the signature.

ROSMÅLNING Traditional Norwegian style of decoration based on canvas scrolls and usually executed in vivid colours.

SKANK SKÅP Dresser-type cupboard with several doors, usually richly decorated.

STÄNKMÅLNING Spatter painting giving a granite-type effect. In Sweden this is done with hundreds of birch twigs dipped into tinted distemper colours.

'SVEPTA' BOXES Small decorated boxes intended for trinkets, keepsakes and other cherished possesssions.

Further Reading

Fredlund, Jane. *Allmogemöbler*. ICA Bokförlag Västerås, 1977.

Fredlund, Jane. *Målada allmogemöbler*. ICA Bokförlag Västerås, 1989.

Gunnars, Anita. *Korgmålning för och nu*. ICA Bokförlag Västerås, 1985.

Nessle, Lena. *Måla inomhus på gammalt vis*. P.A.Norstedt & Söners Förlag, 1985.

Sjöberg, Lars & Sjöberg, Ursula & Nilsson, Sven. *Stolar*. ICA Bokförlag Västerås, 1993.

Tunander, Pontus. *Dekorativ Målning*. ICA Bokförlag Västerås, 1988.

Index